LIFE IN
ANCIENT ROME

1 A sacrifice in front of the Temple of Juno Moneta, A.D. 312

From a reconstruction by J. Bühlmann and A. von Wagner

LIFE IN
ANCIENT ROME

By

F. R. COWELL

Illustrated from Drawings by

D. STREDDER BIST

A PERIGEE BOOK

Perigee Books
are published by
The Berkley Publishing Group
A division of Penguin Putnam Inc.
375 Hudson Street
New York, New York 10014

First Perigee printing, 1980

The Penguin Putnam Inc. World Wide Web site address is
http://www.penguinputnam.com

Library of Congress Catalog Card Number: 75-18629
ISBN 0-399-50328-5

Cover design by Sam Salant

Printed in the United States of America
23   24   25   26   27   28   29   30

PREFACE

A BREATH-TAKING spectacle confronted any traveller in the first four centuries of our era as he approached the city of Rome. A vast number of houses, great palaces, temples, public buildings, monuments and shrines, of a splendour and magnificence with which no other city in the then known world could compare, stretched as far as the eye could see.

Throughout that long time and for nearly two centuries previously as well, Rome had been the chief city in the western world, continuously enriched by the spoils of war, by tribute and by vast profits which came from controlling the destinies of other lands and peoples. It was the centre of the Roman Empire and of civilisation. The wealth of some of its rich men and of its rulers was fabulous. Much though they lavished upon the elegance, luxury and adornment of their homes; freely though they indulged in any whim and in every imaginable extravagance; largely though they were forced to spend upon a misplaced charity to sustain and amuse vast feckless mobs of idle poor, many of them nevertheless spared much also of their fortunes to embellish the city itself.

At the outset, the great difficulty at once occurs of deciding to which particular period the story should relate. Just as nobody would try to describe the vanished everyday life in London without deciding whether to take the London of the Anglo-Saxons, Normans, Plantagenets, Tudors, Stuarts, Hanoverians or Victorians, so it would be impossible to give even a tolerably adequate impression of everyday life in ancient Rome without relating it either to the early primitive days of the Kings in the fifth century B.C. and of the Founding Fathers of the Republic in the heroic days of the fourth, third and second centuries B.C., or to the later time of troubles during the fierce civil wars of the first century B.C., or to that long period of the four succeeding centuries of the Roman Emperors, the great period when the might of Rome rose to ever new heights only to weaken in the third and fourth centuries and to collapse irrevocably in the fifth century A.D. On whatever period we try to concentrate the limelight through the mist of ages, the scene will always be found to shift and change. Much as the Romans liked to think of Rome as something fixed and eternal, they were increasingly conscious of these changes which as time went on, the more reflective among them found more and more reasons to deplore. The story is of such perennial fascination that nothing less than an outline of it as a whole, however sketchy, will be attempted here.

These brief indications may serve to show the settings and the limits of the account here attempted of the main qualities or features of everyday life in Ancient Rome, as it developed from the rustic simplicity of the farmer-soldiers of the early Republic down to the sophistication which flourished, as never before, in a heyday of glory under the Antonine Emperors in the second century of our era.

By continually glancing backwards and forwards in this way, it should be possible to savour something of the changing quality of Roman life, and to realise the full meaning of such well-worn proverbial sayings as 'Rome was not built in a day' and of Virgil's much-quoted line about the epic achievements of his countrymen:

Tantae molis erat Romanam condere gentem
'So vast a toil it was to found the State of Rome.'

January 1961   F. R. COWELL

A number of minor changes have been made in this seventh impression, particularly to relate coinage and measurements to the metric system.

August 1972   F. R. COWELL

CONTENTS

LIST OF ILLUSTRATIONS

The numerals in parentheses in the text refer to the
figure numbers of the illustrations

9

ACKNOWLEDGMENT

The Author and Publishers wish to thank the following for permission to reproduce the illustrations appearing in this book:

Fr. Alinari and the Mansell Collection, for figs. 17 and 25.

The Ashmolean Museum, Oxford, for figs. 18–22.

The Trustees of the British Museum, for figs. 64–7.

Istituto Italiano d'Arti Grafiche and the Museo Nazionale, Naples, for figs. 24 and 55.

Musée Départmental des Vosges, Epinal, for fig. 50.

Photo Ellebé, for fig. 51.

Photo T. C. P., for fig. 76.

Rheinisches Landesmuseum, Trier, for fig. 16.

Figs. 52, 56, 68 and 77 are reproduced from Giuseppe Gatteschi *Past and Present Rome*, by permission of Peter Owen Limited; fig. 75 from Paul Bigot *Rome Antique au IVème Siècle*, Vincent, Fréal et Cie; and figs. 1, 2 and 3 from J. Bühlmann and Alex Von Wagner *Das Alte Rom*, Franz Hanfstaengl (Munich).

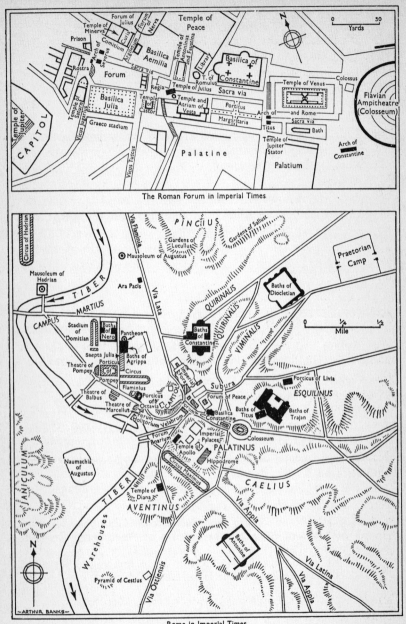

The Roman Forum in Imperial Times

Rome in Imperial Times

Chapter I

THE CITY OF ROME

THE RISE AND GROWTH OF THE CITY

'ROME, Goddess of the earth and of its people, without a peer or a second' amazed the ancient world. Its astonishing history was the story of the growth of a small collection of village huts of the eighth and seventh centuries B.C. into the vast metropolis of the first century A.D. onwards, which in some of its aspects was more splendid than anything that had been seen on earth before or has since been seen. Not in all its aspects however, for together with great magnificence always went stench, inconvenience and far too much abject poverty and squalor.

Generations of school children have been made to pore over the plan of early Rome, to learn the names of its so-called 'seven hills' and of the ancient main drainage sewer, the *Cloaca Maxima*. All this has been learned by children in England who could not name the hills of London or say where the Fleet River reaches the Thames. Six of those seven hills, the Capitol, Palatine, Caelian, Esquiline, Viminal and Quirinal, ringed round a small depression or valley which in the earliest times must have been a swamp. Somewhat to the south of this ring lay the seventh hill, the Aventine. To the west of them all flowed the river Tiber, yellow with sand and mud, and over beyond on its other bank was a longer range of hills, the Janiculum.

By the beginning of the fifth century B.C. the little villages that had gradually formed on the Esquiline, Palatine and Quirinal had grown and united into a more compact community, enclosed by the defensive wall attributed to the King Servius Tullius (578–535 B.C.) although it was not built until after his reign. By that time four distinct divisions or regions of the City seem to have been distinguished: Suburana, Esquilina, Collina, and Palatina. The people living in each of these districts probably considered that their own particular little area was in a very real sense the heart of Rome, their own familiar part of the town

13

with its own special qualities and characteristics, rather as a Parisian is strongly attached to his *quartier*. The walled protection, the so-called Servian Wall, enclosing these four regions, was almost five and a half miles long.

Gradually the tree-clad slopes of the seven hills were thinned and cleared, as the wooden huts were slowly replaced by single-storied houses of brick and tile, above which stood out one or two temples, crowned by a larger Temple to Jupiter, the father-god of Rome, on the Capitol. These temples gradually became old and dilapidated while all the time the low houses were spreading around them and all over the seven hills, so that for pasture land you had to look beyond the four regions, far beyond the walls out to where the corn was grown, and to where olives and vines began to be planted. Slowly the deeply rutted lanes and alleys were given a better surface by being systematically relaid with gravel from the Tiber.

Generations of Roman men, women and children lived and died without seeing any very startling changes in their relatively primitive way of life with its home-grown food, its home-made clothes, and simple furnishings. The old Etruscan temples of the sixth century with their terra-cotta decorations had been patched and repatched. Constant warfare in Italy had left the Romans with little spare energy or resources, and, as long as the idea before them was to be true to the habits of their forefathers, nothing but the necessity of making essential repairs drove them to renew or to rebuild. There was no very significant change in this slow and monotonous addition of huts and simple one-storey houses until the third century B.C. Thereafter the scene began to change with ever-increasing momentum. The wars with Greece in south Italy and the conquest of Sicily in the first Punic War fought against North Africans from Carthage (264–241 B.C.) first brought large numbers of Romans into contact with the architecture of Greece. So impressed were they by its grace and charm that, without giving up their traditional types entirely, they began to build one or two modest temples in the new style of architecture. Greek statues of amazing beauty, which no other Mediterranean people except perhaps the Etruscans had ever learned to create, began to be brought to Rome as booty of war.

A tremendous set-back occurred between about 250 B.C.,

when there had been some 300,000 Roman men citizens over 17 years of age, and 200 B.C., when the number was down to 200,000 or less. The second great war with Carthage had taken a heavy toll. But recovery was swift. As Roman wars spread to the Middle East and as, in the second century B.C., Roman military might proved to be overwhelming in its drilled, trained, organised strength, a steadily increasing flow of booty was brought to Rome. Some local improvements also occurred. Around the middle of the second century B.C. the number of male citizens was well over 300,000, so the total population of the Roman State, now spread over most of Central Italy, men, women and children, must have been nearly a million. About this time a discovery was made not far from the city which provided Roman builders with a new and excellent limestone much harder than the tufa stone with which they used to build. Larger and more solid buildings, temples, arches and bridges could be undertaken using this travertine that may to this day be seen in later buildings such as St. Peter's at Rome which was largely built from stone first hewed by the ancient Romans.

The great Marcian aqueduct was built in 144 B.C. to bring new water supplies to the city. The first stone bridge across the Tiber dates from the same period (142 B.C.). The gravel roads and paths in the City were relaid with stone and volcanic lava brought from the neighbouring Alban hills, once fierce volcanoes. By this time the need hitherto universally felt, to live within protecting walls and gates, had been forgotten; houses had long since spilled over the ancient boundaries of the four regions to cover wider and wider stretches of suburbs which in turn became part of the City itself. The crowds in the narrow alleys and the throng in the centre, the Forum (p. 18), got denser and busier.

Not merely were more and more houses going up but, as will be seen in a later section, some were becoming more spacious and luxurious than anything hitherto within the reach of private citizens. Yet there was still much squalor and poverty in the first century B.C. which must have been greatly aggravated by the long period of civil conflict leading to the collapse of the Roman Republic and the reconstitution of the State by Augustus. When peace came at last, men again had confidence to invest in building. Augustus reorganised the city into 14 regions. In A.D. 6 he formed the first police-force and fire-brigade that Rome had known, the *Cohortes Vigilum*. They were recruited from freed-men who were given full citizenship after six years' service. Each cohort, about 1,000 men strong, looked after two city districts. They were equipped with axes, buckets and some not very efficient leather hoses and hand-pumps, but, as later tremendous conflagrations and bitter complaints were to show, they were unable to rob Romans of their terror of frequent fires. The proud claim of Augustus that he had found a city of brick and left one of marble was exaggerated, but there can be no doubt that the peace and prosperity made possible by his rule led to much building and rebuilding.

The pace had been set and the example given, so it is not surprising that many of the Emperors who succeeded Augustus as head of the Roman State far out-did his more modest though dignified beginnings. The most impressive developments did not occur until later and were not in full swing until the first century A.D. had begun. By then the city probably contained about a million inhabitants.

Building and rebuilding always went on, sometimes from sheer necessity, as when the famous fire of A.D. 64, through which Nero is reputed to have strummed his lyre and recited his poems, had literally rubbed out much more than half the City. This was not the first disaster, as in previous centuries also Rome had been ravaged by fire and by earthquake. Romans never forgot the capture and burning of their city by the marauding Gauls who descended upon them in vast hordes at the beginning of the fourth century B.C. Great fires occurred also in 213 B.C. and again in 192 B.C. when earthquake shocks persisted for a month. The narrow crowded streets and alleys, the large amount of wood in the frames of the buildings and in their roofs, all made a house on fire a great hazard, often completely beyond the power of the urban cohorts to arrest.

After the disastrous fire in A.D. 64 only four of the 14 city regions survived intact. Three had been completely obliterated and seven others hopelessly damaged. The Emperor Nero (A.D. 54–68) then built himself a Golden House in a park so spacious and so magnificent that the malicious rumour circulated that he had started the fire in order to clear a site for it. Another opinion is that he wanted a wholesale clearance of the old shoddy buildings and narrow winding streets so as to reshape

Rome on a clear ground plan such as he had seen in many Greek cities. At any event he breathed a sigh of relief after the destruction was over and his new palace was ready. 'At last', he is reported as saying, 'I can now begin to live as a man should.' After Nero's death Tacitus described Rome as that part of the City not occupied by one man's house. So when a later Emperor Titus (A.D. 79–81) completed the great amphitheatre begun by his father Emperor Vespasian (first of the Flavian line, 69–79) in the grounds of Nero's palace, one of his admirers said that he had given Rome back to Rome. Nero is credited with a great scheme to widen the narrow little streets of the City, across many of which it seems to have been possible for neighbours on opposite sides of the road to shake hands from their projecting balconies on the upper stories. He did not get much gratitude because there were complaints that his wider streets left Romans exposed to the glare of the sun which ground floor dwellers previously could rarely have seen. He cannot have completed the work because Juvenal, two generations later, was still complaining about narrow winding streets. Street names do not seem to have been generally displayed; houses and shops were not numbered, so it was very difficult for strangers to find their way about the city.

An era of peace and prosperity combined with much more public building was made possible by the efficient, economical way in which the first two Flavian Emperors managed the Empire. It was continued by Domitian (A.D. 81–96), the brother of Titus, until he became vicious and indulged in a brutal reign of terror which drove his wife to connive at his assassination. Thereafter began the golden age of the Roman Empire under the Emperors Nerva, Trajan, Hadrian, Antoninus Pius and Marcus Aurelius (A.D. 96–180). Grand and glorious edifices were then added to the City so that buildings, markets, baths, temples, tombs, amphitheatres, gardens, triumphal arches, roads, statues and other monuments accumulated in Rome, until it had attained a splendour and a magnificence which made it truly a wonder of the world. Perhaps no city before or since has ever so captured the admiration and the imagination of mankind.

Few of the millions of visitors who in modern times have thronged the ruins of the Forum in which Cicero spoke and where the body of Julius Caesar was burned, who have gazed spellbound at the mighty Colosseum or stood amazed under the vast dome of the Pantheon, can conceive the full form of the city as it stood complete and intact, humming with life and activity at the end of the fourth century A.D.

The *Forum Romanum* (2) was the great centre of attraction, for it was there that the Roman people had traditionally gathered since the first village settlements on the seven hills. There were few great occasions in Rome's history that had not some close association with the Forum. There were to be seen under the famous Black Stone, the tomb of Romulus, the traditional founder of the City in 753 B.C.; the sanctuary of Venus, the Purifier, where Virginia was killed by her father; the Temple of Castor and Pollux, honouring the twin Gods who announced to the Roman people the great victory they had won with the Roman army in a momentous battle with the Latins in 484 B.C.; and the golden milestone, the centre of the Roman world from which all the miles were measured on all the roads that led to Rome. Deafened by the noise and scared by the great throngs of people, the visitors would be shown the Rostra from which all the great public figures of Rome had spoken. There the body of Julius Caesar had been shown to the people and there the hands of Cicero had been fixed after he in turn had been murdered by Mark Antony and The Caesarians.

APARTMENTS AND HOUSES

Just as thousands today, who could live elsewhere, deliberately choose to be in or near London, New York or another great city, so people responded to the lure of Rome. After the first century A.D. there was no comparable city anywhere in the world: Athens and Alexandria undoubtedly had a great deal to offer, but they were much smaller. As the world-centre of political and administrative life, as the source of social distinction, as the creator of new styles and ways of life, Rome was unique. The urge to live in Rome drove up all prices and increased the cost of living. 'In Rome', said Juvenal, 'you have to pay for everything. Everybody dresses above their means, sometimes at someone else's expense. It's a universal failing; we all live here in pretentious poverty.' But moralists denouncing all the evils and inconveniences of life in Rome probably got the sort of answer Samuel Johnson gave to a critic of London life

18

2 Part of Constantine's triumphal procession (after his victory at the Mulvian Bridge in A.D. 312) passing through the *Forum Romanum*. In the background can be seen the Colosseum and, to the right, the Imperial palaces on the Palatine

in the eighteenth century: 'No, sir, when a man is tired of London he is tired of life; for there is in London all that life can afford.'

The difficulty of providing housing for all the people who wanted to live in Rome forced the Romans before Imperial days to adopt the same sort of solution that prevails today in a city such as Paris or New York. Few except the rich could then live in a town house or detached villa. The great majority were housed in blocks of tenements or apartments usually not more than three or four stories high. Early in the Empire, Augustus put a limit of 70 feet on the height of houses because of their rather shoddy construction. The builders probably sought to economise on bricks. As time went on the Romans made much more use of their excellent lime-mortar in building walls and floors. It sets so hard that it has often been mistaken for modern concrete.

By the end of the Republic the wealthy and notable families who owned their own homes were converting them into very elegant mansions. Some were truly palatial, being richly decorated with marble columns, marble floors and walls, and lavishly provided with curtains and elegant furnishings in ivory, bronze and rare woods. Their general plan was the same, a series of rooms built round an inner courtyard or a square or rectangular basin, the *atrium* (*4*), and another series of rooms built round an adjoining second courtyard or garden. They seem to have been usually bungalows all on one floor, but sometimes the bedrooms were on a second floor. This form of construction was developed in Republican days. The earlier Roman version of it was the single courtyard with the low roofs of the four sides sloping gently downwards over the courtyard which they did not completely cover but left a gap for rain water to fall into a basin and for smoke to escape from the domestic hearth.

When the Romans became richer they added a second house to this *atrium*. It was on the Greek model and was called the *peristylum* (*12*), meaning the part of a building enclosing a courtyard surrounded by columns on the inside. In the larger houses of the rich and in country towns such as Pompeii, this courtyard became a garden. In Rome many of the well-to-do had to be content with roof gardens on a sun-terrace perhaps having fruit trees and fishponds on it. The bedrooms of the family, the domestic shrine, the hearth and kitchen, the dining-room and book store or library, if the owner had any literary interests,

19

3 Part of Constantine's triumphal procession passing the *Tabularium* (the Public Record Office) and ascending the steps of the Temple of Jupiter Capitolinus. In the background are the Imperial palaces and temples on the Palatine, and, to the right, the *Circus Maximus*

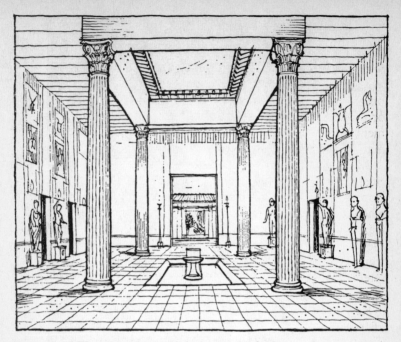

4 The *atrium*, or central courtyard, of a Roman house

were in this *peristylum*. The *atrium* then became the reception
hall where the wealthy owner received, at his morning *levée*, the
stream of his obsequious clients; its smaller rooms might then
be used as offices. The outer walls of such houses were usually
without windows, though some had small ones. In a city which,
like London, had no police force until quite late in its history,
security against marauders was very necessary. The huge doors,
bolted and barred and always guarded by slaves and perhaps
a fierce dog, are another indication of the need for precautions.

Apart from the houses of the very wealthy on the Palatine
Hill, which was increasingly taken over for Imperial palaces
during the Empire, and from the villas of the well-to-do on the
banks of the Tiber and in suburban areas, the great majority of
Roman dwellings were to be found in the apartment and tenement houses in the less fashionable districts of the City. These
were strictly utilitarian, mostly made up of small rooms often
built over shops and having shuttered windows on the street

or on an inner courtyard. Later in the Republic and throughout the Empire, these apartment houses became so large that they filled an 'island' site being bounded on all four sides by streets. Such a block was called an *insula*. Around A.D. 350, a count was made showing that Rome then contained 44,173 *insulae* but only 1,782 private houses (*domus*). Tenants could buy a floor or a room outright, but it was more normal to rent an apartment. Speculative builders and people with money to invest made good incomes by letting rooms, which were not cheap.

After Julius Caesar had returned from the Civil Wars to celebrate his victories in five separate great triumphal processions, it is recorded that he gave 'a year's rent in Rome to tenants who paid 2,000 sesterces or less, and in Italy up to 500 sesterces'. Rents in Rome were therefore about four times as great as in the country. At the same time he gave each of his veteran legionaries 24,000 sesterces 'by way of booty'. The annual interest on that lump sum, if carefully invested, would just about pay a year's rent for a modest room in a cheap apartment house in Rome or it would buy outright a much better home in a country district. 'If you can tear yourself away from the games in the Circus you can buy an excellent house at Sora, at Fabrateria or Frusino for what you now pay in rent for a dingy garret in Rome in one year', said Juvenal. These small towns were near Cicero's birthplace, not more than sixty miles south-east of Rome. Naturally many people paid more than ex-soldiers for larger well-built apartments in a good part of the City, and we hear of rents of 30,000 sesterces a year for a third-floor apartment, which, however, Cicero said was three times as much as it should have been.

The convenience of most of the houses and apartments, judged by our standard, was not very great, although there were improvements in the later Empire. It was not until then that even the more palatial houses were well heated. Roman central heating was then achieved by providing spaces under floors and in hollow walls in which the smoke and heat from a fire in a cellar space beneath could circulate(5). Throughout the Republic and the first and second centuries A.D. Romans had nothing but open charcoal braziers(9) in their rooms so that they suffered considerably in their short sharp winters. Marble walls and stone or marble floors must then have been an

5 Hypocaust system of central heating

affliction to bare feet in sandals. The upper stories had wooden boards. The wealthy contrived to have one of their dining-rooms facing south to benefit from whatever heat the winter sun might give. No rooms, as far as we know, had fireplaces and chimneys except possibly a few kitchens. It was quite late in Imperial days also that thick, opaque glass began to be used for windows. Unless some semi-translucent sheeting of alabaster or other thin material filled the gap, a wooden shutter which blocked out the light was the only way to close a window.

Roman bedrooms seem to have got very stuffy, particularly in winter. Pliny's tip was to disguise the stale smell by burning bread. Water was laid on in lead pipes from the great public aqueducts, but only for the well-to-do, because the users had to pay for it according to the size of their pipes. Martial, who lived a middle class life, said that 'my house complains that it is refreshed by no drop of water although hard-by, the Marcian aqueduct babbles in my ears'. It was not uncommon for Romans to try to escape payment by diverting supplies surreptitiously through pipes of their own, sometimes with the connivance of the labourers of the waterworks who were suitably bribed. Sumptuous private houses from the end of the Republic onwards had lavishly decorated bathrooms, so that the rich owner and his family did not need to join the crowds in the public baths, although many did so for the gossip and society they got there. The lavatory seems usually to have been near the kitchen in order to be close to the water supply of the house.

How the tenants in the *insulae* fared in these respects is far from clear. Many probably had to bring water from a fountain and to resort to a common lavatory on the ground floor or to the public lavatories in the streets; and to public baths (a place in which to get warm in winter), just as they had to go to commercial bakeries and cook-shops for bread or hot food. Slops and sewage tipped out of upper windows into the street below was an unpleasant aspect of everyday life in Ancient Rome which did not lack a parallel in London or Edinburgh until relatively recent times. 'There's death from every open window as you pass along at night', lamented Juvenal, who said: 'You will be thought a fool if you go out to dinner without having made your will.' 'Look at the height of that towering roof from which a pot cracks my head whenever some broken leaking vessel is pitched out of the window.' Rather than that, 'you pray in terror that they will do no more than empty their slop-pails over you'.

Life was by no means free from fearful risks when the poorer Romans were within the four walls of their tenement rooms. Buildings wear out and in Rome many of them had a notoriously short life because of their shoddy construction. 'We live in a city largely shored up on slender supports', Juvenal complained. Danger from falling buildings was a real obsession. So was the risk of fire. 'The place to live in is where there are no fires', said Juvenal, who knew the perils of cheap lodgings. 'Already your third storey is smoking, you yourself know nothing of it for if the alarm begins at the bottom of the stairs, the last man to know there is a fire will be the one who is protected from the rain only by the roof tiles.'

FURNITURE

In comparison with modern times, the Romans hardly had any furniture. They lived more as the Japanese do in bare rooms with a minimum of equipment. Changes in the contents of the average Roman house from Republican to Imperial times there certainly were. In the 'Middle Ages' of Rome, as in England, the prized possessions of a Roman would have been, apart from essential clothing and simple frame beds and couches, a collection of rough agricultural implements: spade, mattock, scythe, sickle, hammer, hatchet, knife, rake, hoe and plough, and weapons of war: short sword, shield and lance. Women would have had their spindle, weaving frame, a chair or stool, grinding stones or mill and some rough earthenware and metal cooking utensils. Women's personal knicknacks in these early days would have been few and simple: a comb of wood or bone, a ring and large brooch or two, some bone or metal hair-pins, perhaps a bracelet or two and some ear-rings kept in a simple trinket box made of terra-cotta or boxwood, and a polished metal mirror. The children would have a few simple toys and games.

In the so-called 'Golden Age' of the Roman Empire, some 300–400 years later, the picture would be very different. Gone are the small huts and houses and with them have disappeared the weapons of war and the farmers' tools. To find spindles and weaving frames it would be necessary to look in the slaves' quarters of a few large houses, although here and there one or two families priding themselves on keeping up ancient traditions might still have a few. In the attic hovels and cramped quarters of the poor, nothing would have taken the place of this honourable traditional equipment. Martial, scornful as Romans were of poverty, describes a removal: 'there went along a three-legged truckle bed and a two-legged table and with it a lantern, a bowl and a cracked and leaking chamber-pot. The neck of a flagon was lying under a brazier green with verdigris and there was a stinking jug.' Such, with the addition of some ragged bed-coverings, a few knives and spoons, drinking vessels and perhaps a worn old chest or two, made up the main belongings of thousands of impoverished Romans.

The higher Romans climbed in the social scale, the more they spent on furnishing their homes, but the money did not go so much upon a quantity of possessions as upon better quality goods. 'Your by no means large amount of furniture costs you a million, a pound of silver runs away with five thousand, you buy a gilt coach at the price of a farm, Quintus', said Martial. Fortunes were spent upon small tables of rare wood and ivory of fine design. Cicero spent half a million sesterces on a single table. On the interest alone of such a sum at five per cent, a man like Martial or Juvenal would have lived in modest comfort. Cicero's

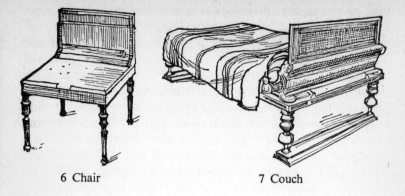

6 Chair   7 Couch

friend Asinius Pollio is said to have spent twice as much on a table. The value came from the rareness of the wood, cypress or cedar for example, and from the fact that the table was cut in a single section at the root of the tree where it exhibited exceptionally fine graining or 'flower'. Chairs(6) were not the ordinary, everyday affair that they are with us. To be seated was traditionally a matter of dignity and ceremony appropriate to magistrates, to judges and to women. Guests too were invited to be seated as a matter of politeness. Children at school, sedentary workmen such as cobblers, patrons of cheap inns(59) all had small round wooden stools, but in the home, men would usually recline on a couch(7). Folding stools were, however, common. Chairs with backs and arms were rarer and reserved for women, the aged, and honoured guests. Late in the Republic and throughout the Empire, portable sedan chairs were in general use. Some held two people. Those for ladies were covered until the first century A.D. when conservative opinion was shocked to see some women being carried around in open chairs. Such contraptions were later than the more usual litter (42) with its six or eight bearers (four was a sign of poverty: it was the number carrying a pauper's bier).

Eastern people, who used to say that the Greeks did not know how to make a comfortable bed, would have thought less of the beds of the early Romans. Theirs were simple, rather high, wooden frames on which a straw or wool-stuffed mattress rested upon girths of leather or webbing with head-boards and foot-boards at the ends. The coverings were a simple blanket or two, or a toga, and there would be a pillow stuffed with wool. Later, as furniture became more elaborate, beds and couches became more richly decorated, of rare fine wood adorned with ivory, tortoise-shell and gold. The coverings of the rich also became magnificent. Infants had cradles, rocked by a girl slave. Beyond making sure that all their essential equipment of this practical kind was as brightly polished, as beautiful and as elegant as possible, wealthy Romans did not fill their rooms. Some had libraries (pp. 166–8), but more mundane tastes were mostly in evidence, and resources went into decorations and display. Martial refers to a man with 'an elaborate sideboard loaded with silver and gold plate', to 'crystal cups brought by a fleet from the Nile', to a man whose friends, 'like his pictures and cups, are "genuine antiques"'. Artists were kept busy painting walls of living-rooms and mosaic workers laid floors, often with consummate skill. They were in great demand because the Romans did not cover their floors, in the Eastern fashion, with carpets. It was just as well, because their table manners were primitive and no carpet would have long remained fit for use in a Roman dining-room. Rich oriental rugs and draperies, no thicker than the average blanket, had been imported long before Imperial times and they were used for curtains and bedspreads.

The charcoal-burning braziers(9), which were the main source of comfort against the cold, were of elegant design and work-manship in richer homes, where the family did not need to congregate round the kitchen hearth—if there was one—on which there were usually some hot embers if not an actual blaze. If the fire went out and the embers were dead, it might be quite a business to get it going again. The first resource would be to beg a flame from a neighbour—then as now, the poor were great borrowers—'a flame, water, the knife, the hatchet, the pestle and mortar, things neighbours are always trying to borrow', says a man in a play by Plautus. If that failed it was necessary to produce a spark to light dry tinder, touchwood, leaves or sulphur. Failing a flint and steel, the recipe, according to Pliny, was 'to rub and grate one wood against another, and for this intent there is nothing better than to strike ivy wood with bay'. For light at night, lamps burning olive oil were the stock resource from very early times. They were simple flat saucers of earthenware(8) with a handle at one end and a spout

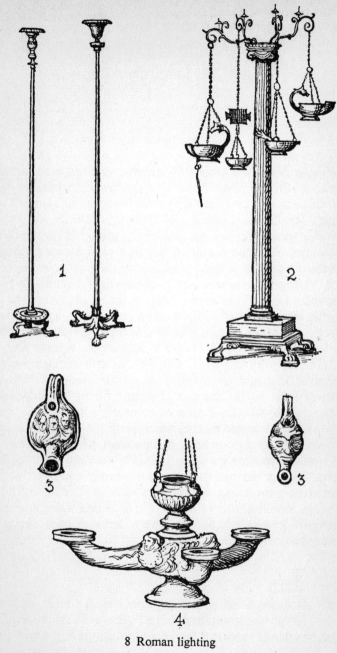

8 Roman lighting

1 Silver candlesticks   2 Bronze lampstand
3 Terra-cotta lamps   4 Hanging lamp

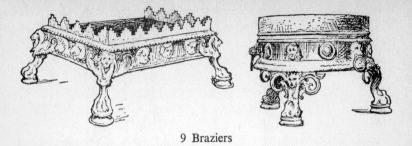

9 Braziers

at the other from which a wick emerged made from twisted fibres of flax or papyrus, to hang downwards so that, when lit, its flame would cast light downwards as well as in other directions. Mr. O'Dea, in his *Social History of Lighting*, records that a test made on such a single-wick lamp provided between 40 and 50 hours' light for a pint of oil. In a poor Roman home this expense would have been grudged, for olive oil cost money and it was a food. The more wicks, the better light, but also the greater expense. One of the grand lamps with as many as 14 wicks, would, as Martial says, 'light up an entire feast with its flames', but none but the rich could afford it often. Candles made from tallow fat rolled round a twisted wick were a Roman invention used mainly by the poor, but with careful economy because tallow also could be eaten. The age-old tradition of cheese-paring economy in the use of light, still by no means dead among those who have no need to practise it, dates from these early times. A single candle, which is all that many households would afford, gives a poor light, except near the flame. One electric lamp of only 60 watts gives a hundred times as much light. A hundred candles placed around a room nevertheless would be more effective than one such electric lamp, but few Romans could afford so many. Early to bed was a sound rule for most Romans, but there were exceptions such as the men whom Martial scorned:

> *Let the o'er sour and dull that way delight*
> *Whose lamps at midnight see the wretches write.*

All such open-flame lights greatly increased the risk of fires to which Rome was so exposed, but a light was badly needed in the tight-shuttered rooms in which people stumbling about in the dark might have some accident or inadvertently desecrate the little shrine of the household gods. The Romans knew of the existence of crude oil or petroleum, called either *bitumen liquidum* or by its Greek name of *naphtha*, 'which is so very inflammable', said Pliny, 'that nobody makes any use of it'.

In addition to the rare and costly gold and silver cups, dishes, and other vessels adorning the loaded sideboards of the rich (64–7), they would own a full service of silver spoons, the Romans' main, if not only, article of tableware, for knives and forks or prongs were used in the kitchen and not at table. Food was eaten with the fingers or with spoons. Small spoons with a sharp-pointed handle were used by guests to extract snails and shell-fish from their shells while their small round bowls at the other end served when eating eggs; larger spoons more akin to our dessertspoons met all requirements for which fingers were inadequate.

At first cups and dishes were mostly of earthenware (*10*) as none but the rich could afford metal such as bronze, silver and

10 Earthenware cups and dishes

29

gold, and such luxuries were considered ostentatious. Romans, like the Greeks, had no word for a plate in the modern sense, hence the need for bread and napkins and slaves with bowls of wine and water and sponges to clean greasy fingers and tables between the courses. Drinking horns(70) were of immemorial antiquity and with the advance of civilisation they became elaborately carved, chased and mounted with silver, gold and gems. Cups of every sort were to be had, from the tough 'dread-nought' type, *calices audaces* of the plebeians 'not cracked by boiling water', to the crystal: 'so long as you fear to break them you will', as Martial said of the Murrine cups from the East, which may have been porcelain, so very costly they were—Nero having paid a million sesterces for one. All other kinds of earthenware utensils, moulded, engraved and plain, were to be had, as well as those of silver by an ancient Greek master silver-smith and the chased and inlaid gold and silver ware of later times, collected and prized by the well-to-do.

Domestic brooms made from wild myrtle, tamarisk or palm twigs and brushes made from all manner of things such as Martial advised ('if your clothes were soiled with yellow dust let this light ox-tail put them right with a gentle flap'), 'barbarian baskets from woad-stained Britons', buckets and water-carriers of earthenware or bronze were all to be found among the utilitarian equipment of the home.

During the late Republic and throughout the Empire it would be in the ladies' apartments rather than in those of their husbands that evidence of great wealth would be most apparent(11). Golden rings, bracelets, bangles, anklets, ear-rings, pins, buckles, brooches, necklaces, hairpins, fillets lavishly bejewelled and of exquisite workmanship, spilled in lavish profusion from precious caskets which were jewels in themselves. Rows and rows of little pots of alabaster, marble and rare stone contained priceless perfumes and essences. Far outdoing the modest attirements of the middle classes, the gorgeously arrayed women of the richer homes carried personal adornment to heights as great as have ever been known. These aspects of luxurious living are mentioned here although they will again be referred to, because they point to a change of the utmost significance in the Roman way of life, a change that finds illustration in many other aspects of every-day life. It was a change the Romans themselves noticed and many deplored, without however doing anything much to alter their own way of life. Before it happened, Ennius, Rome's first poet, could proudly boast at the end of the third century B.C. in the spartan days of austerity of the Republic: 'Rome stands four-square upon the well-tried way of life of the men of old.' Two hundred years later Horace, looking at the changed manners of the men and women around him, asked 'what does ravaging time not devour?', and said 'our parents' age, worse than our grandfathers', has brought us forth less worthy still, to produce offspring yet more wicked'. So the luxury and refinement in home and furnishings so briefly sketched above have a deeper significance which it will be well to bear in mind. Some efforts were made by more responsible rulers to check the tremendous increase in personal extravagance and luxurious living by laws

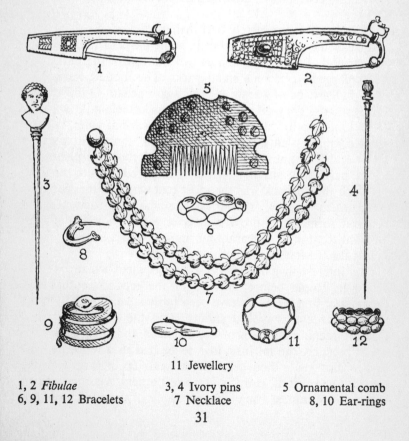

11 Jewellery

1, 2 *Fibulae*	3, 4 Ivory pins	5 Ornamental comb
6, 9, 11, 12 Bracelets	7 Necklace	8, 10 Ear-rings

limiting expenditure on meals, the amount of silver a man should own or the amount of jewellery a woman should wear, but they all failed, for, as Horace summed up the wisdom of ages: 'Of what avail are mere laws if we lack principle?'

GARDENS

Romans made considerable efforts to remain in contact with nature because many liked to think of themselves as country-folk exiled in the City. As time went on, however, a new race of people began to fill the tenement houses who inherited no such ancestral attachments to the soil. Indeed, the very idea of living in the country made many slaves and freedmen shudder. For them and their forebears the country held hateful memories of ceaseless hard toil, often in those chained gangs that Plautus in the second century B.C. described as 'the iron-bound race in the country'.

The very rich not merely had their roof-gardens, their inner garden of the peristyle(*12*), but in some parts of the City they had grounds round their houses which a few of the immensely rich enlarged to become small parks. The models were those Eastern 'gardens of paradise' which so enchanted the Greeks and Romans. They offered a delightful spectacle of grass, trees of all kinds both ornamental and fruit-bearing, vines, ivy and other creeping plants, flowers, a fountain, some statuary or a shrine and some animals and birds, particularly doves, pheasants, ducks, partridges and the gorgeously coloured birds of the East, of which the peacock was the most renowned. Some would be wild, others in cages or aviaries. The whole was designed and laid out formally to provide at once a pleasure to the eyes, pleasant scents and a pleasant murmur of water, bees and birds, except for the harsh noise of the peacocks.

This interest in gardens was a development which had not begun in Rome before the end of the second century B.C. Progress at first seems to have been fairly steady. Although the feelings gardens provoked sprang from the new unrestrained pleasure-seeking impulses of the Romans and their desire for social prestige, the intrinsic joys to be had in a well-cared for garden also made their perennial appeal. To literary men like Cicero, Ovid, Virgil, Horace, Pliny and others, a garden was an invaluable stimulus. The old mystic sense of some religious link

32

12 A peristyle

between man and the powers of nature persisted. There were many gardens across the river Tiber frequented by all the best people in Rome. Another great garden area on the City side of the Tiber, and a garden, much of it remains to this day, was on the Pincian hill. Two of the largest and most famous of all Roman gardens were there, the garden of the great general, and exceedingly rich, Lucullus, on the west, and the garden of Sallust on the eastern side.

During the Empire the scene changed rapidly. The growth of the City population, and the consequent demand for a multitude of tenement buildings, obliterated many private houses and their gardens. The greed of Emperors and their womenfolk absorbed some of the best that remained, particularly those on the Palatine hill. The huge gardens amassed by the Emperor Nero were split up again when he was killed. Despite these ups-and-downs of fortune, many gardens survived, to provide a greater proportion of open-air space in Rome than has remained in London or in Paris. In Rome, as in modern cities also, the high cost of building in the centre of the City led to a great expansion of suburban building, and there it was easier for the wealthy to include a garden with their homes.

While the rich had their gardens or their roof-gardens, the poor in their tenement rooms in the barrack-like *insulae* had to rest content with their window-boxes and pot-plants. 'The common people of Rome, with their miniature gardens in their windows, offered to the eye a reflection of the country', said the Elder Pliny, although he speaks as though this was no longer as true in the first century A.D. as it once had been, for he added, that in his day 'the vast number of shocking burglaries compel us to shut away such sights from passers-by with bars'.

Chapter II

GROWING UP IN ANCIENT ROME

THE strength of any country, and more obviously of primitive communities, depends directly upon its manpower, so, from the earliest times, Roman boys were badly needed to plough, to cultivate the crops and to fight when their people were attacked. Daughters, after the first, were thought a disaster. Human life was not regarded by the early Romans as something sacred, to be preserved at all cost. They were ready to kill at birth any weakly, malformed, diseased, sub-normal or even surplus healthy infants although, before they did so, five of their neighbours had to examine the child and to agree with the parents' sentence of death.

Such ruthless ways of controlling the growth of the population are to be found among many primitive communities. Although the Romans remembered these and other survivals of their prehistoric past, they had long given up the savage practice of exposing unwanted children to be eaten by dogs or wild animals. The ancient tradition which permitted such a practice was never forgotten and throughout the history of Rome, until the coming of Christianity broke with the pagan past and introduced the new idea of the sanctity of human life, there were no legal or moral rules to restrain human brutes from killing their children or from leaving them to perish. Discord between man and wife, acute poverty and all manner of reasons might lead ill-disposed parents to get rid of an unwanted child. Death was merely one of the risks to which the miserable infant was exposed and it may have been a more merciful end than to fall into the hands of the slave-trader. For, although according to Roman Law a free-born child abandoned by its parents could not be reduced to slavery, the child would often have no knowledge of its origins and no opportunity of invoking the law even if it were to become aware of it. One of Rome's most ancient legends tells how the founder of Rome and its first King, Romulus, together with his brother Remus had been abandoned to perish in the River Tiber and how both were saved by a she-wolf who reared them as she would have done her own cubs.

This same Romulus, who was supposed to have made the law that the Romans should preserve all their sons although they need not care for more than the eldest of their daughters, is said to have decreed at the same time that nobody should kill a child under three years of age. A delay of three years gave the parents time to get a good idea of the real nature of the child, and, human nature being what it is, parents who had cared for infants for three years would not lightly cast them out to die.

Following a very ancient tradition of the Indo-European peoples a solemn ceremony was held either at home or in a temple nine days after a boy was born; eight days after a girl was born. The child was then 'consecrated' or 'purified' and a round or heart-shaped lucky charm (*bulla*) was hung round its neck. The charm would be of gold when the parents were rich and of leather if they were poor. It was supposed to ward off all evil influences. Boys wore this charm until they came of age at around 14–16 years. Girls kept it until they were married. This was but one of the superstitious customs which the Romans inherited from the Etruscans and always preserved. It was at this ceremony that the child was given a name. In very early days two names sufficed, but after about 300 B.C. a boy got three names, *nomen* the name of his clan or gens (Cornelius or Tullius, for example), preceded by his first name *praenomen* (Publius or Marcus) and followed by the name of his family *cognomen* (Scipio or Cicero). The full name of Rome's greatest orator was Marcus Tullius Cicero. In official lists it would appear with the first names of his father, grandfather and greatgrandfather as well as the political division in which he was registered: *M. Tullius M.f. M.n. M.pr. Cor(nelia tribu)*. Girls were known by the feminine form of the name of their gens or clan, followed sometimes by the name of their father's family in the genitive; thus Cornelia Scipionis would be the daughter of a Cornelius Scipio. Cicero's daughter was known as Tullia, although her father, who adored her, called her his little Tullia, 'Tulliola'. A girls *praenomen* in later times, such as Gaia or Lucia was a feminine form of a boy's first name. Names are sometimes confusing, particularly in an old and well-established aristocratic

36

family where many of the boys were given their father's first name: Cicero's son was also called Marcus Tullius. In indexes and books of reference the family name is used for men, the feminine form of the clan name for women.

The Roman tradition required the parents to train all their children whom they decided to bring up in the world—*ut omnes liberos susceptos educarent necesse est*—but it also left the children completely in the power of their father. Just as he would have been able to kill them at birth, so he retained the power of life and death over them as long as he was alive, after which his eldest son himself became supreme judge of the family fortunes. Such powers extended beyond instant obedience to any commands, however difficult, unpleasant or dangerous. The father might sell his son to be the slave to another man or have him killed. According to the Roman historian Valerius Maximus, A. Fulvius, a senator, had his son executed for joining the camp of Catilina who was conspiring to overthrow the government of Rome in the last years of the Republic.

Such ferocity had by that time become something quite abnormal, to be explained only by the intense fear of civil war, but the story is worth recording as evidence of the tremendous power over life and death traditionally regarded as being within the right of a Roman father. Suetonius records, as though it were nothing unusual, that, in the reign of the first Emperor Augustus before the end of the first century B.C., 'owing to a disagreement between his parents' Gaius Melissus, a free-born child, was disowned by his parents, but found a protector who brought him up, gave him a good education and then made a present of him to the Emperor's rich friend Maecenas. But, although Maecenas appreciated him and treated him as a friend and although his mother tried to restore his freedom, 'he yet remained in a condition of slavery'.

Much of what we know about training children in the early Republic comes from the few writings that remain of the Elder Cato (234–149 B.C.), always known as the Censor, who sought hard to maintain the practices of his forefathers. To throw a spear, to fight in armour, to ride a horse, to box, to endure heat and cold, and to swim the most rapid rough rivers—these and other manly exercises such as running, jumping, fencing were the first essentials, pursued not as gymnastics or as a 'keep fit' routine but in preparation for the real business of life on the battlefield with the Roman legions and in the fields where the Roman people then got their living. Cato added reading, writing and arithmetic (for he had sound business instincts), law, public affairs and particularly Roman traditions. For this latter purpose he is said to have written out for his son in large letters a simple history of Rome.

From the very earliest days of the City, Roman children would be brought each morning to reverence the goddess of fire, Vesta, at the family hearth. Of immemorial antiquity, this homage to the mystery of fire was deeply ingrained in the Roman soul. No religious body was more reverenced in Rome than the Vestal Virgins who tended the symbolic sacred fire in that small temple whose ruins are still plainly visible in the Forum of Rome. This band of priestesses almost certainly developed out of the ceremonial ministrations of young daughters of the home at the family hearth. The fire cooked the food taken from the larder or store-cupboard guarded by the *Penates*. These protecting spirits were not alone, for each house had its *Lar familiaris* (13). To fight for *Lares et Penates* was to fight for hearth and home; for everything that was most sacred and precious in life. That there should be many such protecting spirits brought comfort to the Roman soul and no effort to fit them all together into a connected intelligent scheme of religious beliefs or a theology seems to have been felt necessary. At an impressionable age Roman

13 *Lararium,* or shrine of the *Lar familiaris*

children would be daily witnesses of the honour paid to the hearth and to the household gods; they would have seen their mother in anxious prayer at a crisis in the fortunes of the family or of the State; as soon as they were able, they also would join in such devotions; they would have their own petitions to make and they would make them in unquestioning obedience to the practices taught them by their fathers and mothers. The girls were trained by their mothers to undertake all the responsibilities of a housewife, so that when the daughters themselves became wives and mothers they would acquit themselves well. To keep the fire tended, to fetch water, to prepare food, to cook, to spin and to weave the homespun yarn and to make it into clothes for the family were traditionally the duties of a Roman matron. For centuries they were handed down from mother to daughter with little change. They formed the picture of the ideal Roman woman of the Republic long after many Romans had become rich and were served by armies of slaves who undertook all such tasks.

In the same way in this early period the boys were taught to follow in their fathers' footsteps and to prepare for the life that he had led as a farmer, as a soldier and maybe as one of the City elders who had been elected to serve for a year as a magistrate. If their father was or had been one of these leading political figures such as a consul or praetor, he would be visited early every morning by large numbers of people seeking his advice and help in their own affairs. Boys would sit beside their father, listening to their clients and to the advice their father gave, and, no doubt, to his comments afterwards when the clients had departed. They also accompanied their father when he went to speak in public and sometimes when he was invited to dinner by friends and neighbours. They shared the family table, they helped to serve the food and drink, and after the meal one of them would say that the share of it offered to the household gods had been acceptable to them. At solemn religious ceremonies and at family funerals they were also impressionable witnesses.

SCHOOL AND SCHOOLMASTERS

Before the end of the Republic the education of many Roman children had been handed over to schoolmasters. A school exercise described a Roman schoolboy's day in Imperial times like this:

Before it is light I wake up, and, sitting on the edge of my bed, I put on my shoes and leg-wraps because it is cold. Then I take a clean towel. A slave brings a jar of water which I pour over my hands and face and fill my mouth with it. After rubbing my teeth and gums I then spit it out and dry myself properly.

Taking off my nightshirt I put on my tunic and belt; I put oil on my hair, comb it, wrap a scarf around my neck and put on my white cloak. Followed by my school attendant and my nurse I go to say good morning to daddy and mummy and I kiss them both. I find my writing things and exercise book and give them to a slave. I set off to school followed by my school attendant. I say good morning to the school friends whom I meet and they say good morning to me. Arriving at the entrance I climb the stairs without making a noise. I leave my cloak in the hall and quickly comb my hair.

I go into the schoolroom and say 'Good morning master'. He kisses me and returns my greeting. The slave gives me my wax tablets, my writing things and ruler.

'Hello fellows, let me get to my place, squeeze up there. Come out! That's my place, I had it before you.' Then I sit down and begin to work. When I finish learning my lesson I ask the master to let me go home to lunch. As he lets me go I wish him well as he does me. Reaching home I change, take some white bread, olives, cheese, dried figs, and nuts and drink some cold water. After lunch I go back to school where the master is beginning to read. He says, 'Let's begin work.'

At the end of the afternoon I'm off to the Baths with some towels with my slave. I run up to meet the people going to the Baths and we all say to each other 'Have a good bathe and a good supper'.

Before the end of the Republic in the second and first centuries B.C., many Roman boys and girls had got used to a routine of school life just like this, which went on with little change throughout the next four centuries, except that during the Empire they had the Baths to go to in the afternoon, as the above quotation shows. It also shows that children rose early. Romans pitied the poor boys and girls whom dawn robbed of their sleep, handing them over to the schoolmaster to be caned. 'You cursed schoolmaster, what right have you got to disturb us before the cock crows with your savage threats and beatings?' angrily asked Martial, who lived too near to one of these schools to enjoy a quiet life.

Schools and schooling evidently varied greatly. 'In the training of boys of free birth', wrote Cicero, 'our ancestors (unlike the Greeks) held that there should be no fixed system, laid down by the laws, or set forth by authority, or the same for all.' It was no business of the community as a whole to interfere with the father's absolute power within each family. Romans remained of this opinion; they never developed a national educational system.

A Roman school would often be nothing more elaborate than a one-man school(*16*) in a single room or a small booth, just like a little Roman shop, open to the street and shut off merely by a curtain. From the very scanty evidence we have about Roman school-life it would seem to have been a miserable affair. However much some children today dislike their school-days, there can be little doubt that they would seem heavenly by comparison with the purgatory endured by many Roman children.

The masters also had a lot to endure if we are to believe Juvenal who wrote in the first century A.D. With bitter jest he describes the way in which the pupil's fee, already small, was liable to be nibbled into by the slave who brought it, and urges the schoolmaster to put up with it:

> *While something's left, to pay you for the stench*
> *Of smouldering lamps, thick spread o'er every bench,*
> *Where smoky vapours Virgil's pages soil*
> *And Horace looks one blot, all soot and oil,*
> *Even then this stipend thus reduced, thus small*
> *Without a lawsuit, rarely comes at all.*
> *They'll give thee for thy twelvemonths' anxious pains*
> *As much as, in an hour, a fencer gains.*

Teachers were, in fact, very poorly paid, many of them working hard for no better reward than that earned by any artisan or manual worker. The father of the poet Horace did not want his son to go with the village boys to the local schoolmaster, each taking eight *asses* a month as his fee, but he probably did not have to pay so very much more to send young Horace to the school of Orbilius in Rome. An *as* was a small copper coin and eight *asses* were equal to half a *denarius*. A soldier in the ranks was paid by Julius Caesar at the rate of 225 *denarii* a year but his food, clothes and lodging were provided free. A teacher with 30 pupils would get 15 *denarii* a month or

180 *denarii* a year from which he had to find his own food, clothes and lodging. This was a mean reward even in the days of the Republic when a free Roman would have needed at the least about 250 *denarii* a year if he had a wife to support.

This Lucius Orbilius Pupillus was one of the most famous schoolmasters of the first century B.C. He came from Beneventum in South Italy. His parents had been murdered. After teaching there for many years he moved to Rome in 63 B.C., the year when Cicero was chief magistrate or Consul. He was then 50. His teaching, says Suetonius, gained him more fame than cash. Indeed in his reminiscences (now lost) he admitted that he had been very poor: so poor, in fact, that he lived in a garret 'under the tiles'. Horace immortalised him by the one word 'flogger', apparently with justice, because another victim also testified to his savagery, referring to 'whomever Orbilius thrashed with a stick or leather whip'—evidently they were a numerous brood. His fame earned him a marble statue in his native Beneventum where, says Suetonius, 'he may be seen at the left of the Capitol sitting wrapped in a Greek mantle with a couple of boxes of books beside him'. He lived to be a hundred, a pathetic figure because he had lost his memory. His son, of the same name, followed in his footsteps as a teacher of grammar.

A contemporary of Orbilius, Publius Valerius Cato, who had had many aristocratic pupils and was a very good teacher, also reached an advanced age, to die, miserably poor, in a wretched hovel after having had to sell up his villa at Tusculum to pay his debts. Most of these old schoolmasters seem to have had a hard time and relatively poor rewards, although here and there a few of them were much more successful, particularly in the more prosperous centuries which followed after the time of Orbilius and Valerius. The patronage of the great, particularly of the Emperor, was one way to distinction. Interesting descriptions of these old schoolmasters are to be found in what remains of the *Lives of Illustrious Men* by Suetonius.

As discipline had been harshly enforced in the early centuries of the Roman Republic, ill-tempered and brutal schoolmasters of later times were able to keep up such old traditions without any compunction. They could quote the wisest of the Greeks, for Aristotle had said that 'education certainly ought not to be made a means of amusement. Young people are not playing when they are learning, because all learning is painful.'

Caning on the hand was a regular corrective and stimulant. More severe was the flogging with a leather whip (14). The Romans seem

14 Schoolmaster flogging a pupil

to have believed the often quoted line of the Greek playright Menander (*c.* 342–291 B.C.), whose works were popular in Roman schools: 'A man who has not been flogged is not trained.' Very few voices seem to have been raised in protest but one such was the Spanish-born Quintilian, Marcus Fabius Quintilianus (*c.* A.D. 35–100), who said: 'I have no use for flogging although it is a regular custom, because it is a revolting way of punishing slaves. If a boy is so wooden that he will not respond to reproofs he will merely be hardened by blows, like the worst sort of slave.' In spite of bad treatment, Quintilian thought it better for children to go to school than to be educated at home. But the old tradition of home education persisted and, as Rome grew rich in the last century of the Republic and in the centuries of the Empire which followed, more and more parents provided their children with private tutors, usually Greek slaves, bought in the slave market, where they would fetch a considerable price if they were especially skilled in reading, in music or in arithmetic. As there was no compulsory education in Rome, children might grow up illiterate if their parents did not choose to educate them. There was also no State control or inspection of schools throughout the Republic and early Empire. In the later Empire the most that anxious, interfering Emperors undertook was to exercise some control over teachers and perhaps to encourage municipalities and provincial governors to appoint better or more schoolmasters.

In later times, when the Roman educational system had been fully developed, the great majority of Roman children never progressed beyond the primary or elementary standard, which meant that they learned little more than to read and write and to repeat 'copy-book' maxims enshrining some moral teaching. Some simple arithmetic would probably also have been included —though even this must have been complicated enough. For all Roman numerals are combinations of the six letters I (1), V (5), X (10), L (50), C (100), M (1,000), and the cumbersome nature of this numerical system is evident from the fact that eight letters are needed to express the number 88: LXXXVIII. Multiplication and division, like adding and subtracting, were done by moving beads on a counting frame or *abacus*. But even these small accomplishments had to be won despite the drag of the home environment, where often little regard was paid to learning. Even in the first century of the Empire the child might be more influenced by his nurse or, when he went to school, by the slave who escorted him there than by the schoolmaster. Quintilian urged parents 'above all to see that the child's nurse speaks correctly'. Of course he knew that 'the most important point is that they should be of good character'. But, he said, 'they ought to speak correctly as well'. Like all sensible parents, Romans or others, he thought that influences in early childhood could be both deep and tenacious. Tacitus had the same opinion, complaining that 'nowadays we entrust the infant to any little Greek slave girl, with one or another of the male slaves to help her—usually the most worthless of the whole household', with the result that 'tender and impressionable minds are filled from the very start with these slaves' stories and prejudices, but no one in the whole household cares a bit'.

By the first century B.C. children of middle-class and wealthier parents might look forward to a longer school life when they would leave the *litterator* and go on to study under a *grammaticus* to begin the study of literature. 'As soon as the boy has learned to read and write without difficulty, it is the turn of the teacher of language and literature', said Quintilian. 'I prefer that a boy should begin with Greek', he declared, 'because Latin, being in general use, will be picked up by him whether we want it or not;

44

while the fact that Latin learning is derived from Greek is a further reason.'

Suetonius (A.D. 69–140) sums up the development of literary studies by saying:

> The study of grammar at Rome in early times was not merely regarded with little respect but it was not pursued at all, which is not surprising in those rough and warlike days when there was no time to spare for civilised studies. The subject was begun in a modest way because the earliest teachers, who were half-Greek (I mean the poets Livius and Ennius who taught both languages in and outside Rome), only translated the Greeks or read out whatever they happened to have written themselves in Latin.

By half-Greek Suetonius meant that both Livius and Ennius were Italians who came from the southern part of Italy which had long been ruled by the Greeks. Livius translated Homer's Odyssey into Latin around 250 B.C. A beginning could thus be made in Rome with literary study in Latin, and the Romans were fortunate, when they began to take education seriously, to be able to tap the priceless heritage of Greek civilisation and culture. Few Romans realised their good fortune in this respect because the great majority were concerned solely with the more matter-of-fact affairs of everyday life. So, in the family circle and at school, children would become familiar with Roman ways of telling the time, the day of the month and year; they would learn to recognise money as well as to be able to count and to measure weight, length and volume. Probably it was not until they had left the elementary school of the *litterator* and gone on to study under the *grammaticus*, as the children of wealthier parents were able to do by the first century B.C., that they would be likely to make much progress with sums and simple calculations. Some Roman ways of measuring were not very different from ours, which indeed are remotely based upon them, but others, particularly the calendar, were very different.

TELLING THE TIME

Unless the sun was shining and they were near a good sundial, the Romans never had any way of measuring time with accuracy, so that it was very difficult for a person in one part of Rome to be sure that both he and someone in another part of Rome would give the same answer if asked what hour of the day it was. Being without clocks or watches they had to base their reckoning of time upon sunrise and sunset. These two fixed points of the day, which are the same for everybody, marked the limits of most people's activities because, as we have seen, artificial lighting by oil lamps and by candles gave poor light, needed constant attention and produced much smoke and soot. The Romans, limited as most were by the length of available daylight, divided it up into twelve hours so that midday was the moment when the sixth hour became the seventh hour. Midnight was similarly the moment when the seventh hour began at night. As the days are longer in summer than in winter the Roman hour of daylight had to be longer also, but as they did not try to divide hours into minutes this did not much matter. When we write a.m. for any time in the morning before midday we are abbreviating the Latin words *ante meridiem*, 'before the middle of the day', while p.m. means *post meridiem*, 'after the middle of the day'.

Roman sundials were borrowed from Greece. The first to appear in Rome during the first Punic War came as war loot from Sicily. When it was put up in Rome around 263 B.C., the Romans did not know that a sundial which was accurate in Sicily would not be correct in Rome because of the difference in latitude. It was apparently not until one hundred years later that the Romans discovered their mistake and after that they began to put up more accurate sundials. About the same time (159 B.C.) they began to import water-clocks from Greece. These worked upon the system of regulating the water dropping from one container into another. They might, like the later hour-glass filled with sand, serve to show just the amount of time it takes for a given container to empty itself. Or the water might drip at a known steady rate into a container marked at different levels so that the amount of time which had passed could be measured by the height of the water in the lower container. Later, in Imperial times, they became more elaborate and easier to read, but with the best available advice the Romans never succeeded in measuring the time correctly even when an Emperor tried to do so. Augustus, with the aid of a mathematician (an enthusiast for astronomy, Manilius) made a sundial out of a large obelisk in the field of Mars. Writing about 65 years after the death of

Augustus, Pliny complained that 'for these 30 years past or thereabout the use of this quadrant hath not been found true, and what the reason thereof should be, I know not'. Seneca had already said that it was easier to find agreement among philosophers than between two water-clocks.

Sundials and water-clocks, moreover, divided up the hours of the day into equal parts, and so clashed with the traditional hours of the day which were, as has been seen, of unequal length. They were not much use, therefore, to the average schoolboy or girl or to their parents. In fact time-reckoning and timekeeping was always a hit-and-miss, approximate affair in Rome.

THE CALENDAR

Although the Romans numbered the years, beginning their first year with the mythical founding of the City by Romulus, its first King, in what we would know as the year 753 B.C., they remembered events not by a numbered year but by the names of the two Consuls who commanded the State when those events occurred. To try to make children learn dates in history lessons would therefore be very difficult, for the dating of Roman history was far more complicated than is British or American history, with its divisions by the reigns of kings or the terms of office of presidents, because two Consuls were elected afresh every year and some served more than once. It would tax the memory even of a Macaulay to be able to recite the Roman Consuls in order—as he was easily able to do for the Popes of Rome.

The old traditional Roman year began on the 1st March until, in 153 B.C., it was officially altered to the 1st January. That was the day on which magistrates or the chief officials, newly elected each year, first took up their public duties. In very early times this year was of 10 months only, but in historical times it became one of 12 months.

It is very difficult to calculate the exact duration of one complete revolution of the moon round the earth or of the earth round the sun. Roughly the lunar month is $29\frac{1}{2}$ days and the solar year is about $365\frac{1}{4}$ days. It is not surprising that in early times the Romans went astray in their reckoning and occasionally had to add, or, as they said, to 'intercalate' an additional month. Julius Caesar put that right when he became supreme dictator of the Republic. Luckily the new moon, for which most Romans always had superstitious reverence, occurred at 6.16 p.m. on the 1st January 45 B.C., and Julius Caesar based his reformed Roman calendar of a year of 12 months upon the 1st January as New Year's Day. So much better were the calculations on which his new arrangement was based that his calendar year—the Julian calendar—lasted unchanged in England until 1752, when again there had to be a reform because by then it was 11 days out. Such a change could not have been made except by a resolute man, for the Romans were tenacious of old customs. Even those who probably agreed with Caesar's reform could not resist a joke. Soon afterwards when the great orator Cicero, who hated dictatorship and was broken-hearted at the decay and disappearance of the old Republican Government, was told by somebody that the constellation Lyra would rise next morning, he replied: 'Yes, no doubt, in obedience to Caesar's edict.'

Roman children learned, as the weeks and months went by, how to reckon time and what were the traditional holidays, festivals and ceremonies of their country. They differ so much from ours and they were so intimately part of everyday life at Rome that a look at the Roman calendar is full of surprises. The names of the months, however, were those we still use, except that before 44 B.C. the fifth month was called *Quintilis*. It was then renamed Julius (our July) in honour of Julius Caesar. Similarly August was *Sextilis* until 8 B.C. when it was changed to honour Augustus. Other emperors tried to make similar changes in their own honour, but they did not last.

The Romans did not count the days in the month straight through as we do from 1 to 30 or 31 (or 1 to 28 or 29 for February), but they divided each month up into three parts and reckoned their days as so many days before each of these three divisions, except for February which had a special system of its own. The three dividing days in the months were the Kalends which always fell on the first of each month; the Nones, which in March, May, July and October were on the 7th of each month, but in all the other months on the 5th; and the Ides, which in March, May, July and October were on the 15th but in all the rest on the 13th. Thus, July 4th would be written *IV ante nonas*; 8th August would be *VI ante idus*; 24th February would be *VI ante kalendas Martias* with *posteriorem* added in a leap-year.

48

In the early Republic, as in the Middle Ages in England, money did not much complicate life. Coins were rarely needed. The simpler life of the Roman farmers was largely self-sufficient. They grew their own food, bred their own cattle, made their own houses, clothes and rough implements. If they needed money to buy land or an ox, or for some ceremonial occasion such as for a daughter's dowry, or wedding present, they counted out some rough metal bars of copper or bronze on which had been stamped the likeness of an ox or cow. There was then little foreign trade and when it was not some form of barter it would be in the hands of relatively few men. Business grew gradually as city crafts and industries became specialised and took over work done at home. Shortly after 300 B.C., three round coins came into more general use: the *as*, a large heavy coin of about 10 oz., the *semis*, one half the size of the *as*, and the *uncia*, one twelfth the weight of the *as*. These coins were based on the duodecimal system which British children used, before the metric system, for sums in shillings and pennies or in feet and inches. 12 is useful as a multiple because it can be divided easily into three or four parts leaving the whole numbers 4 and 3. This cannot be done when the scale is based on 10, the decimal system, as on the American dollar or the new English coinage.

15 A banker

This early system of the Romans was ruined by the disastrous war, in which bronze had to be used for weapons to fight the Carthaginians from North Africa under their brilliant commander Hannibal. He all-but wrecked the Roman Republic, and the rest of Italy as well, until he was vanquished in North Africa in 202 B.C. by Scipio, who was henceforth called Scipio Africanus in honour of his great victory. Not until they had made good the damage done to the Italian countryside were the Romans able to profit by the defeat of their greatest rival in the Mediterranean. As they succeeded, they steadily grew richer, and, with the increase of commerce, bankers(15) began to play an important part in Roman life. Not very long after 200 B.C. the old bronze *as* was replaced as a standard coin by a new silver coin called the *denarius*. After some minor changes, Roman money from about 123 B.C. was mainly reckoned by two silver coins, the small *sestertius* and the *denarius*, which was worth four *sestertii* and was slightly smaller than the English silver 5p. Its name survived in the '*d*' of the British *L.s.d*. With the Empire came the gold *aureus* worth 25 *denarii*. The old copper *as* was then struck again, 16 *asses* making one *denarius*. A quarter of an *as*, the *quadrans* or 'farthing' was also issued. It was an insignificant little coin but it gave admission for one day to one of the great *thermae* or Baths. Later emperors resorted to the odious practice of robbing the public by putting less valuable metal in the coins than their value declared them to possess (*18–20, 22*). People soon found out; prices rose, ending in a financial catastrophe in the third century A.D.

WEIGHTS AND MEASURES

Roman school-children must have found their weights and measures just as complicated as present-day equivalents seem to school-children now, and it is unnecessary to mention here more than those in most general use which will be referred to on other pages of this book. The Roman pound (*libra*) was made up of twelve ounces, each weighing about one British ounce (28·35 grams). The Roman foot (*pes*) was just over $11\frac{1}{2}$ inches (31·75 cms), their pace (*passus*) of five feet, the nearest measure to the yard, was therefore 4 feet $10\frac{1}{4}$ inches (1·48 metres) and a thousand of them measured a Roman mile which was 1,618 yards (1,480 metres) instead of the 1,760 yards in a British mile.

The most common measure of land, the *iugerum*, supposed to be the area a yoke (*iugum*) of two oxen could plough in a day, was five-eighths of an acre (2523·34 square metres).

Wheat, salt and similar commodities were measured by the *modius*, nearly one peck (8·732 litres). Liquid measures were the *hemina*, one-twelfth of a congius of about 5¾ pints (3·275 litres), so that one British pint is roughly the same as the Roman.

HIGHER STUDIES

It is not likely that much time would have been spent on tables of weights and measures in the grammarian's school because its one main and severely practical purpose was to prepare boys for advanced studies under a teacher of public speaking, the *rhetor*. These higher studies were valued because they were a means of achieving a successful career as a pleader in the courts of law, and so of entering the race for political and administrative distinction. Few Romans had any use for mere literary study. They had conquered the world without relying upon rhetoric, literature, philosophy, astronomy, Greek poetry and drama, so at first any suggestion that Roman boys should study them was frowned upon. Yet the demands of Empire and world trade were growing and the need for Greek was insistent.

Greek was not merely the key to treasures of thought, learning and science to be found in no other language; it was also the language through which the Romans had to deal with the provinces which their armies had won for them in southern Italy and Sicily and in the eastern Mediterranean lands. It was, moreover, the common universal language for trade and business in Egypt and of course in Greece itself. To know Greek thus became a sign of some social distinction, as it has been ever since, rather in the way that a knowledge of French would distinguish an aristocrat in eighteenth-century or early nineteenth-century England or Russia, or a knowledge of English spread among the educated classes in the nineteenth century in Asia, Africa and elsewhere.

So educated Romans, unlike the Greeks and unlike most early peoples, had to learn to use a second language. Such was the competition to succeed in public life that a long and careful training was essential. This meant that none but the richer families would be able to send their boys to a more advanced school to study the art of speaking with elegance and true persuasive power. There was no fixed age for this change, so Quintilian's simple formula was probably as good as any, that a boy should leave the grammarians and go on to learn rhetoric 'as soon as he is fit'. 'As a rule', he said, 'boys are almost young men by the time they go to the teacher of rhetoric and they stay there when they are indeed young men.'

The three stages of Roman education were therefore very roughly equivalent to our primary or elementary education, to secondary or grammar school education and to a University career, although it is dangerous to suggest any such analogies, because in Rome everything was done on a small scale by private enterprise and there was nothing remotely like our vast elementary, secondary or university buildings, staff or curricula. The range of learning open to children and young people was restricted in comparison with our present-day schooling. Not all Romans exposed to Greek cultural influences were able to profit by them, so those who succeeded became yet further apart from the children of the Roman poor or middle class who, unless they were exceptionally gifted and exceptionally lucky, would never attain personal intellectual distinction.

It was long before the Romans realised the need for higher studies. The Elder Cato, in the second century B.C., had a sound, simple rule for teaching his son to be an orator: 'Stick to the point', he said, 'and the words will come.' Suetonius records that in 161 B.C., 'as a result of a discussion in the Senate, it had been decreed that philosophers and rhetoricians be not allowed to live in Rome'. The Roman way for a gifted boy to get a start in life was to serve as an apprentice, as it were, to a prominent, successful public figure, if he did not have a father able to guide him. Cicero, when a young man, was attached to the old and wise Pontifex Maximus, Mucius Scaevola, one of the elder statesmen of the early first century B.C. from whom he learned the main principles of statecraft. Old suspicions about schools of rhetoric persisted.

It was about this time (92 B.C.) that the two Censors, Crassus and Domitius, high officials with a special duty towards public morality and good behaviour, declared:

It has been reported to us that there are men who have introduced a new kind of training . . . as Latin rhetoricians and that

16 A schoolroom scene

The schoolmaster is reprimanding a pupil who has arrived late for class. The other two pupils are unrolling their papyrus-rolls

17 Interior of a shop selling belts and pillows

Two shop-assistants, watched by the shop-owner, open a box with a pillow inside it for two customers, who are seated on a bench and attended by their slaves

young men spend whole days with them in idleness. . . . These innovations in the customs and principles of our forefathers do not please us or seem proper. Therefore it appears necessary to make our opinion known both to those who have such schools and to those who are in the habit of attending them, that they are displeasing to us.

We do not know whether much notice was taken of this pompous stuffy statement, for, as so often with public moralists, these views were considerably out-of-date. Advanced studies in Greek and Latin had become popular among the upper classes of Rome during the two previous generations and they were not easily displaced. People with specially strong cultural interests, such as Cicero, sent their sons to Athens for training, so great in the intellectual world was the reputation of all things Greek.

But, although the study of rhetoric became established as the only kind of formal higher education open to wealthy young men, a dismal picture is given by Seneca and Tacitus of the quality of much of what passed for higher education in the Roman schools of the rhetoricians. It was all very well for Quintilian, who was one of the best teachers, to make great claims for training in oratory, pointing out that 'the art of writing is connected with that of speaking, and faultless reading precedes interpretation'; that 'every kind of writer must be studied carefully not for the subject-matter alone but for the vocabulary, for words often acquire authority from their use by a particular author', and to go on to show that music must be understood if metre and rhythm were to be mastered, not to mention astronomy and philosophy. Many instructors were incapable of doing justice to such undoubtedly sane requirements, so that Seneca could complain with only too good reason that 'we waste our efforts on the inane. We are educated not for life but for the schoolroom.'

Tacitus was even more sweeping on the subject of the schools of the rhetoricians. Of the students attending the average such establishment he said: 'It would be hard to say what is the most prejudicial to their intellectual growth, the place itself or their fellow students or the studies they pursue.' They were supposed to be trained in the art of persuading and of controversial arguments, 'but good heavens, what poor quality is shown in

53

18, 19 (obverse and reverse) Tiberius. Twin grandsons on horns of plenty; titles of his son Drusus   20 Nero   21 Galba   22 Galba   addressing troops

SOME COINS OF THE EARLY EMPIRE

(All these coins are brass sestertii, *reproduced to a scale of* $1\frac{1}{2}$: 1, *except for figure 21 which is a gold coin, twice its actual size)*

their themes . . . in addition to a subject-matter so remote from real life, there is the bombastic style in which it is presented'. He gave as examples of the themes proposed: 'The Reward of the Tyrannicide' or 'The Ravished Maid's Alternatives' or 'A Remedy for the Plague'. Yet a generation earlier Seneca had suggested topics such as: 'Alexander the Great deliberates whether he should enter Babylon after he had been warned of danger by a soothsayer', or 'Cicero deliberates whether he should burn his writings since Antony promises that he will be unharmed if he does'.

Too great an importance cannot be placed upon the titles of college exercises set by tired tutors forced to try to find new and stimulating topics year in and year out, but the prospect of great intellectual stimulus arising from such exercises as these can hardly be thought very exciting. As Tacitus remarked, it would be difficult to expect young students to be capable of the maturity of judgment that many of the controversial topics required. No doubt there were other less futile examples, but in a time of Imperial absolutism or despotism, such as prevailed for the greater part of Rome's history after Julius Caesar, free discussion of political questions such as individual liberty or democratic rule would have been as dangerous as it is today in communist prison-States.

From even this short account it is evident that energies to improve the intellectual and moral fibre of the Roman people were by no means fully engaged. Education was valued for its practical help in day-to-day activities. Literature and oratory were judged by their power of helping a man to win a lawsuit or to sway an electoral mob. Music was good only in so far as it inspired or was able to quicken some manly activity such as fighting. The Greek idea that an educated and cultured life is a good thing in itself because it implies some degree of active desire to discover the truth, to appreciate and to achieve beauty, as well as to attain to morally worthy conduct in human relations, did not appeal to many of the down-to-earth Romans.

Chapter III

FAMILY LIFE

THE SPIRIT OF HOME LIFE

'THERE is nothing more holy, nothing more securely guarded by every religious instinct than each individual Roman's home.' Such, said Cicero, was the tradition of the fathers of the Republic and it was long maintained. However, the average Roman home would not have seemed a very comfortable place to us, but this did not matter to many Romans who, in Imperial times at least, preferred to spend most of their day outdoors, strolling, gossiping, at the Baths or the Circus, Amphitheatre or theatre. Then they came home to their dinner, the main meal of the day. It would be a family affair for most of them and after it there would be little time except in summer to go out again before dark when it could be dangerous because of bullies and robbers in the narrow alleys and the heavy wheeled traffic which, by Julius Caesar's orders, was allowed in Rome only at night.

No contemporary picture or account of a Roman family at home has remained, no novel, letter or play to give a vivid feeling of the personal relations within a normal family circle. There are accounts of one or two grand dinner parties and occasional flashes on the family scene in the letters of Cicero, who had two children, and of Pliny the Younger, who had none and was a grandee with literary enthusiasms and not therefore very typical. From these and other chance remarks we get pictures of Roman life which are often contradictory. The predominant impression that the Romans were dignified, serious folk deserving respect rather than affection is confirmed by some Greeks whose quick, sympathetic, affectionate nature and whose love of beauty and reverence for cultural excellence stood in marked contrast with the dour, matter-of-fact Romans. 'At Rome no one ever gives away anything to anybody', said Polybius in the middle of the second century B.C. Almost three hundred years later, another Greek, the tutor of the future

Emperor Marcus Aurelius, said that there was no word in Latin to express the tender affectionate love of parents for children that was conveyed by the Greek word *philostorgos*. You never met in Rome, he said, a man to whom the word could be applied and he did not believe such affection existed in Rome. And this was at the close of that period which Gibbon declared 'without hesitation the most happy and prosperous in the history of the world'.

These learned Greeks exaggerated, for it would be false to the record to pass over evidence, as time went on, of a growing sensitive insight, a deeper human emotion and a genuine urge and longing for better things. The devotion of husband and wife, their affection for their children, for their slaves and for their pets, stands out in many a page of Roman literature and on many of the tombstones and memorials that have survived into modern times. Tombstone inscriptions may perhaps be suspect as reliable evidence, but they are echoes of what can be found in Roman literature. Lucretius, writing about the close of life, could say: 'Now no more shall your glad home welcome you, nor your good wife and sweet children rush to snatch the first kisses and to touch your heart with a silent thrill of joy.' Quintilian, who lost first his young wife and then his two sons, all of whom he adored, writes about them in poignant words of grief which pierce the centuries that divide us from him. But he was a Spaniard.

Tibullus has a pleasant little picture of a small child taking hold of his father's ears to snatch a kiss and of an old grandfather always ready to watch by the child's side and to prattle with him. There was plenty of fun also in Roman homes. Cicero speaks of Laelius and Scipio revelling in the country, collecting sea-shells and generally enjoying themselves.

Cicero, whose care and affection for his two children must strike anyone who reads his letters, declared in his book *On Duty* that the foundations of society are the bonds of union first between husband and wife and next between parents and children. 'Our parents are dear, dear are our children' because, he believed, 'nature implants in man above all a strong and tender love for his children'. Certainly he was no ruthless mercenary father to his own son and daughter. On the contrary, as he realised when it was too late, he had been too busy with his career and public affairs to give them all the attention they needed and had perhaps spoiled them by over-indulgence. In ordinary households things were probably different. Occasional glimpses of Roman children show them at school or helping their parents in the daily tasks of life in the house, field and farm. Such is the vivid picture Virgil presents of the boy who very early fell in love with the little girl next door whom he saw early in the morning picking up apples in the orchard with her mother. Scrappy as such indications are, they suggest that there was much in Roman family life that would seem quite normal to us, today, at least as far as the boys were concerned.

How about the Roman girls and their mothers upon whom then, as today, the task of creating a family circle and a true home mainly depended?

WOMEN AT HOME

Long before historical times two forms of marriage had been practised in Rome. One, *coemptio*, was a form of wife purchase, and it was at first observed mainly among the lower class of plebs. The other involved a solemn religious ceremony performed by two senior priests, the *Flamen Dialis* and the *Pontifex Maximus*. This was marked by the exchange of wafers made from wheat and was called *confarreatio*, and was strictly binding for life, divorce being practically impossible. The aristocracy or patricians of early Rome mainly observed this form of marriage. The difference between the two forms has been thought to indicate that the patricians were descended from the early invaders of Italy who came from the Teutonic north and who bequeathed a strongly marked oral tradition of matrimonial fidelity.

Marriages by bride-purchase had some religious flavour, for three copper coins, *asses*, were brought by the bride, two of which were given to the household *lares*. The bridegroom kept the third. It was a symbolic dowry. The Goddess Juno was supposed to lead the bride to her new home. After the bride in her red veil had joined hands with the bridegroom (*23*), a victim had to be sacrificed to Jupiter. The bride's hair was parted into six strands by a spear-shaped comb. She was accompanied to her new home by a gay procession and after anointing and adorning the doorposts, she was lifted over the threshold. The

23 Wedding ceremony

bridegroom presented her with fire and water. Then there was a feast, which would usually be enlivened by bawdy songs and comments. A poem by Catullus remains to give a good impression of a Roman wedding during Republican times. But these grand ceremonies were soon to become things of the past. A third and purely civil form of marriage, *usus*, became general throughout the Empire. It was held to occur when a man and woman lived as man and wife for a year. It was a looser bond, such as might at first be thought to befit people whose social standing was not considered to be very important. A woman would not be legally bound by it if she spent three nights in the year away from her husband.

The lot of girls and women in very ancient Rome would seem today hard, and often harsh. Her arrival in the world was often a sign for mourning, as it has long been with the Chinese. If she was brought up at all she might not be treated much better than a slave. Catullus, who was violently swept off his feet by his intense love of a young Roman matron, uses, in speaking of the feelings of parents towards an unmarried daughter, the strong word '*invisa*' which had no other meaning than 'hated' or 'detested'. The most that many a poor girl could hope for was to be less detested after being married off to some fellow her father had found for her. For she, with the rest of the family, was completely in her father's power. If he found her a husband she would be entirely cut off from her own family and completely under the equally absolute rule of her husband or of his father, if he were still alive. If unmarried, she could be sold as a slave. Marriage as an institution was very different from what it has been in modern times in Western Europe, partly because the law and practice in ancient Republican Rome left a woman without legal rights in a world in which men both made the laws and carried them out. Partly also the profound difference resulted from the great and increasing number of slaves flooding into the City as a result of successful wars. Among them would be some pretty young women and their numbers were increased by piracy and high-handed action in Rome's dependent territories which were steadily growing larger. Rome was not the only land where women were held cheap, and parents elsewhere, like the Chinese in modern times, readily sold their daughters. A wife therefore faced severe competition in her own house where all the women slaves were just as completely at the mercy of her lord and master as she was. Roman women even in early times had plenty of spirit and were ready to stand up for themselves. They put up with a wartime law, passed in 215 B.C. after Rome's dreadful defeat by Hannibal at Cannae, forbidding them to own more than half an ounce of gold, to wear coloured clothes and to ride in a two-horse carriage. Five years after the war was over the women were tired of austerity, but men of the old school, Brutus and Cato, would not hear of repealing the law. So 'the women could not be kept indoors either by the authority of the magistrates, the orders of their husbands or their own sense of propriety. They blocked all the streets to the City . . . and besieged the doors of the two Brutuses who were preventing the repeal.' The women won and the law was abolished.

Legally, however, women remained in a miserable condition of dependence, from which they were slowly redeemed. Perhaps advancing civilisation saved them, although it had not redeemed Greek women, but it seems more probable that they were really rescued by their own strength of character, aided by the development of the dowry. It was the well-to-do families who had a stronger interest in the sanctity of marriage, through their desire to perpetuate the family name, to maintain family rites and ritual on behalf of the spirit of their house, their household gods and the shades of their ancestors, as well as to ensure the due and legitimate transmission of the family's wealth and possessions. These pious duties could not be discharged if the head of the family took up with a succession of slave girls who had neither legal nor religious standing. Well-to-do families began to seek distinction and to take pride in providing their daughters with a substantial dowry. The consequence was profound. No longer did the husband of a dowered wife have her completely in his power. Her father, who had found the cash, was not going to let it go without remedy in case the marriage turned out badly. He therefore retained his father's rights over his daughter.

Already by the time of the early Empire, the ancient form of marriage by *confarreatio* had become almost unknown. None but a few of the oldest families kept it up, and they were dying out fast. The dowry strengthened the wife's position because, if her husband neglected her for the girls of the household, she could complain to her father and put the marriage in jeopardy. As soon as the old religious marriage ceremony was given up, it became just as easy to cancel a marriage as to contract one. The religious penalties had gone, but a sharper economic penalty took their place, and it was more feared, because if a marriage was cancelled the dowry had to be repaid. The husband did not receive the dowry if his father were still alive, for a son had no independent rights to property and could not therefore go to law about it. Until the days of Augustus even a man's army pay belonged to his father. As children could legally become engaged at the age of seven and as they could be married as soon as the girl was 12 and the boy 14, there cannot be much doubt about the complete power of the parents over their children's marriage. Romans were married and remarried at their father's whim until the days of Marcus Aurelius towards the end of the second century A.D., when the father's power to break their children's marriages was diminished. They did not lose it completely for they might still dissolve a marriage if they could prove that they had an abundantly 'just cause' and it would always be easy to find such an excuse. A son could, however, break his marriage, although his wife could not. The husband's father, as long as he lived, had absolute power over all his grandchildren also, so the parents had no legal rights over their own children until the

24 A baker and his wife

From a Pompeian wall-painting of the first century, A.D.

grandfather died. By making a traffic out of their daughter's marriages, Roman fathers showed what a low consideration was put on marriage as an institution: it was nothing for a Roman to remarry three or four times.

The fear of being called upon to restore the dowry was one hard reality which might put a brake upon a ruthless father or husband. Its consequence was yet more far-reaching, for a married daughter lost her bonds when her father died. She then appointed a legal guardian who was no more than her agent while she controlled her own life and dowry. The result was to put women into a position of independence that they lack in many civilised countries today. They were able to control their own establishment and their own way of life. An elegant mixed society life, to which women give such grace and distinction, became a reality in Imperial Rome, perhaps for the first time in history.

It cannot, unfortunately, be reported that all Roman women in high society used their unexampled new freedom wisely and well. The high rate of divorce has been mentioned; so also in other parts of this book reference is made to their superstitious addiction to Eastern mystery cults, their tendency to 'fall for' successful actors, gladiators and charioteers, and their harshness as employers. They were accused, like the menfolk, of having favourites among their slaves also. Fierce penalties punished such infidelities. An errant matron could be sold as a slave or her father could kill her and the guilty slave might be burnt alive. But the degraded depravity of an Empress such as Messalina typifies the depths to which an abandoned woman could sink despite such laws. The men were just as bad or worse. What we consider as gross immorality was rife and much of Roman society in the early Empire was fundamentally rotten.

ENCOURAGING LARGE FAMILIES

The Romans could never forget their need for manpower; penalties upon bachelors and privileges for the parents of numerous children were the two stock ways of trying to keep up numbers. Augustus in 18 B.C. laid the foundation for Imperial policy in this matter as part of his great plan to reform public morality and to restore something of the traditional virtues of the great days of the Republic. The need for improvement had

25 A well-to-do lady being dressed by her slave girls

From a bas-relief of the third century, A.D.

provoked a short sermon from Horace: 'prodigal of vice, our age has first polluted the marriage-bed, then our children and our homes. Here is the origin of the disasters by which our people and our country are submerged.'

Augustus decided on no half-measures to stop 'debauchery or adultery'. If a father discovered an adulterer of his daughter he might kill him and his daughter with impunity. A husband in similar circumstances could also kill the guilty man, but not his wife whom, however, he had straightway to divorce otherwise he too would be punished. Nobody might marry such a woman, who would in addition lose half her dowry and a third of her property and be banished to an island. The guilty man, if he was not killed, was to lose half his property and also be sent to an island, but, the law sagely commands, not to the same island as his guilty partner. This seems to have been a law for the rich because the poor had no property and would have starved on an island. Another law of Augustus of A.D. 9, in the names of the two Consuls of the year, Papius and Poppaeus, both of whom were bachelors, penalised the unmarried, gave privileges to married people, rewarded those with large families and removed some of the class barriers. 'Since among the nobility there were far more men than women, he permitted free men except Senators to marry freedwomen [i.e. former slaves] and recognised their offspring as legitimate.' Senators and their descendants down to great-grandsons and great grand-daughters were still not allowed to marry freedwomen or freedmen or anyone who had been an actor or whose father or mother had been an actor.

Augustus himself was no saint and he deserved to be a victim of his own laws, as he made his witty and dissolute daughter by his first marriage, Julia. Her scandalous behaviour, despite her father's laws, was the talk of the town. When, very late in the day, Augustus learned the truth, his anger was boundless. Julia was sent to live in privation and isolation on the island of Pandataria. When her former husband Tiberius became Emperor he made her fate yet harsher, so that she died of consumption in solitary confinement.

The only way of taking any action under these and many other Roman laws was upon information laid against the allegedly guilty parties by informers. These vile creatures accordingly grew and prospered until, as Tacitus bitingly commented, 'every household was undermined by denunciations of informers and the country then suffered from its laws as much as it had previously suffered from its vices'.

The laws of Augustus remained unrepealed, but they were openly spoken of as futile and unenforced. Their failure was merely a symptom of the deep-seated malady which all reflective Romans recognised. So the moralists continued to lash out at the women as well as men. On tombstones and in histories, however, many women shine with a purer light. When, in the reign of Claudius, the fatal words of doom were sent to Paetus, his wife, who need not have died, was the first to take the dagger. Plunging it into her breast she pulled it out and handed it to her husband, saying before she fell, 'It does not hurt, Paetus'. When in the following reign a freedwoman, Epicharis, was seized with other conspirators against Nero, she refused under the most fearful torture to give away her companions, while the men were wildly accusing their nearest and dearest in the hope of saving themselves. The old traditions were tough: 'She loved her husband with her whole heart. She bore two sons. Cheerful in conversation, dignified in manner, she kept the house, she made wool.' Such is the conventional picture of feminine virtue under the Republic. The strength of character which such words reveal was a quality which would compel respect even in a manmade society and so go far to counter the theoretically absolute power of the husband in the home.

BEAUTY TREATMENT

Much time could be given to recounting the tremendous amount of time and effort which some Roman ladies gave to their daily toilet and adornment(25), but it would hardly be right to regard it as a matter of everyday life except for a limited number of the rich. The great majority of workaday women then, as today, had little time or resources for such extravagance. They kept up the early Republican traditions of primitive simplicity from necessity rather than from choice. Unlike the rich, they had no little curled and scented poodle dogs sleeping on their silken couches nor were they awakened by a tame parrot crying out 'Good morning! Good health! Bravo!' Poor women were not found lying in bed, their faces thickly smeared with paste made from flour and milk waiting for slave girls to bring in silver or golden bowls of water disguised with scented essences to wash off the mess. In a well-to-do household this preliminary task would be followed by rinsing the mouth, for toothbrushes, toothpowders, and pastilles to sweeten the breath were part of the daily toilet routine. Blackened and discoloured teeth, common among the poor, shocked polite society where very white teeth and false teeth made from a special cement paste, ivory or bone were by no means uncommon. Ovid reminded girls, 'You can do yourself untold damage when you laugh if your teeth are black, too long or irregular', advising them not to open their mouths when they laughed, but to show dimpled cheeks instead. Elegant ladies would take a morning bath for which few other Romans had any facilities, after which they would be rubbed down and massaged. Some might have superfluous hair removed by rubbing with pumice stone, a practice which calls to mind the French saying that beauty is to be had only at the price of pain. But razors and drugs such as bryonia were also used. Plucked eyebrows were accepted as an aid to beauty as early as the first century B.C.

Efforts to preserve and beautify the hair were carried to great lengths by both sexes in the Roman Empire. The most extraordinary concoctions were prepared under the age-old illusion that hair can be made to grow by anointing the scalp with oils, greases or fluids. Marrow from deer bones, fat from animals such as bears and sheep were recommended. One repulsive remedy was made from rats' heads, rats' excrement, hellebore and pepper. In spite of all precautions, Roman men and women continued to lose their hair. False hair and wigs, like false teeth, incited the sarcasm and scorn of those in no need of such aids. The sight of the bald head of a great personage whose wig had been blown off by the wind was thought sufficiently funny to warrant commemoration in verse, just as Ovid could not resist recording that he once called unexpectedly on a lady friend who, in her hurry, put her wig on the wrong way round. 'Women with scanty locks should keep their doors well-guarded' was his advice. Those well-endowed with woman's crowning glory, however, might with advantage, he declared, allow an audience while it was being combed by industrious slaves who would use elegant combs made from boxwood, ivory or tortoise-shell. Curling irons, mentioned by Plautus in the second century B.C., were in general use. Cicero a hundred years later mentioned that some effeminate men also used them.

The great variety of hairstyles (71) was as bewildering during the late Roman Republic and throughout the Empire as it is today and it excited just as much jaundiced comment from some of the men whom it was supposed to attract. There is no specifically Roman, as there was a Greek style, because fashions continually changed. So much so that a sculptor was known to allow for it by producing a sculptured portrait of a Roman lady with a detachable scalp so that it would be kept up-to-date as new hair-styles came into fashion. Young girls and women of good families often tied a white or purple fillet round their heads.

The dressing-table of an elegant woman was covered with rows of pretty little boxes and caskets containing all manner of beauty aids, because face powders, scent and make-up were used lavishly (26). Sometimes they were crudely applied with little taste or skill and some did not stand up to great heat or bad weather, again inviting damaging comments. 'While Fabella, smeared with chalk, fears the rain', said Martial with scant gallantry, 'Sabella's rouge fears the sun.' The tasteless use of heavy perfume caused Cicero to say: 'The right scent for a woman is none at all', but as other Romans knew, it depended

26 Beauty aids

1 Make-up jar
2 Powder box
3 Lipstick
4 Scent bottles

27 Bronze hand-mirror—
back view

on the woman and perhaps the weather, and the frequency of her visits to the Baths. Darkening the eyes and prolonging the arch of the eyebrows with some blackening material were also tricks at which Roman girls were adept. Some stuck black patches or beauty-spots on their faces, particularly if they had some small blemish to hide. Others relied upon a rich display of heavy jewellery to add to their distinction. Some indeed overloaded themselves with a great wealth of heavy gems, whether the occasion for their display was fitting or not. Pearls and emeralds were greatly prized, but diamonds were little used because no way had been found of cutting and polishing the stones. The twentieth century would not have had much to teach Roman girls about the art of personal display, from bikinis to make-up, but the Romans would no doubt envy the modern age for its greater skill in producing beauty-aids and in making many of them available cheaply, for all classes. Among the many modern improvements would be the mirror. The Romans had not discovered how faithful a reflection can be obtained from a film of mercury behind polished glass and they had to rely upon highly polished metal. Their mirrors were mostly small hand-mirrors (*27*), but larger wall-mirrors were also known.

BARBERS

Men would have incurred ridicule and hostility in the early Republic if they had spent much time and effort upon their appearance. In the third century B.C. some Romans began to shave off their beards, but the practice did not become at all general until the great Scipio Africanus set the fashion at the beginning of the second century B.C. The poorer classes then, as today, did not always follow the fashion. Martial, in one of his many expressions of disgust at the habit of Roman men kissing each other on all possible occasions, speaks of 'a bristly farmer with a kiss like a he-goat's'. The poor had a good excuse for not shaving because it was thought to be too difficult, if not impossible, for a Roman to shave himself. Those who had no slave for the job went to one of the barbers' shops that were to be found all over the town. They were great centres of gossip and their scene of operations used to extend across the alley or street outside their little booths until Domitian cleared all shops off the streets. Martial, who records the old danger to the passers-by from the poised razors, also curses a clumsy barber, warning his readers that:

> he who does not yet want to descend to the underworld should avoid barber Antiochus . . . these scars on my chin, if you can count them, may look like those on a boxer's face, but they were not caused that way, nor by the sharp talons of a fierce wife, but by the accursed steel and hand of Antiochus. The he-goat is the only sensible animal, by keeping his beard he lives to escape Antiochus.

Martial also mentions a woman barber in the poor quarter of Rome, the Subura, but he gives her a very bad reputation. Roman razors did not have the keen edge of even the old 'cut-throat' razors which men used before the invention of safety-razors, for the art of hardening and sharpening steel had not been mastered by the Romans, whose lack of coal and forced draught made it impossible for them to temper steel efficiently. So the tyrant of Syracuse who used to singe off his beard with a piece of glowing charcoal may have had other motives than the fear of assassination which is said to have driven him to do so. Young men did not begin to shave until they took the manly toga. The first down then shaved off their young faces was often preserved in a little trinket box and dedicated to one of the Roman gods.

Romans became more 'modern' in the first century B.C. and so most of them remained throughout the Empire, in the sense that they began to believe that the urge to enjoy pleasurable sensations was not merely allowable, but the main aim in life. The old-fashioned way of life of the tough farmer-soldiers with its spartan, self-denying discipline and sacrifice of the individual to the community and the Republic, began to seem more and more rustic and uncouth. Trimmed and ornamental

28 Beards of the second century A.D. (*left*) and the late Republic

beards appeared on the faces of foppish young men to excite the amusement of their elders, such as Cicero, who had a special word for them, *barbatuli*.

Beards came back in the second century A.D. (*28*) because the Emperor Hadrian (A.D. 117–138) grew one to hide some blemishes on his face. They had never entirely gone out because they were the badge of philosophers and they used to be grown as a sign of mourning. However, the revival of beards did not become general or lasting because Romans after Hadrian are depicted on their statues without beards.

CLOTHES

Looking after the average home was mainly a matter of providing enough clothes and food. In the early days of the Republic all clothes were home-made. The striking thing about Roman clothes is how simple they were. They had to be, because the Romans were limited not only by their raw materials, which were at first almost entirely wool and flax, but also by their means of making them up into cloth.

The result of hours of work spinning thread from raw wool and weaving it on a hand loom was a web of woollen thread. It might be of any shape, whether square or rectangular, circular or semicircular. Such a 'blanket' was the basis of all

Roman clothing for men, women and children, for emperors, consuls and slaves. Knitting seems to have been unknown.

Before it could be made up into the very simple garments which the Romans hung or wrapped round their bodies, it had to be cleaned, bleached, combed and brushed, unless it went to make a garment for a workman or a slave, when such refinements, apart from cleaning, were omitted. The simple 'home-spun' of the poorer classes has only very recently disappeared, for up to the end of the nineteenth century it was still very widely used in Great Britain and in the United States. If the Romans had made it with wool straight from the back of the sheep, it would have retained its natural oil and grease, and would have been almost fully waterproof, but the wool thread was usually cleaned before being spun or woven and the clothes themselves when woven were sent to have all dirt and grease removed. This job was done by the fullers, who used carbonate of soda (nitre), potash or the special kind of alkaline clay known from its use as fuller's-earth. Soap was not used for cleaning.

Cleaning clothes could not be done easily in the home. Not that it was difficult, but it wasn't very pleasant and demanded more room, more water and often rather more equipment than the average Roman house could provide. In a wall-painting in Pompeii fullers are depicted at work in large vats, treading the soaking cloth with their feet (29). Washing and treading the cloth in this way and beating it helped to 'mat' it or 'felt' it together and so to thicken it. Ordinary home-spun when so cleaned went back to be made up into clothing or blankets. Finer woollens, which had been more carefully made from finer threads for the more well-to-do, were bleached. The bleaching process was also very simple. The blankets of cloth were draped over large, round wickerwork frames and placed over a small pot of burning sulphur. The fuller's trade had its hazards to health. Breathing burning sulphur is bad for the lungs and treading the cloth in vats full of chemicals day after day was liable to produce skin diseases, particularly when, in their dearth of chemical knowledge, urine from the public lavatories in the Roman streets was used. After bleaching, the cloth was again washed and brushed with a comb, with teasels or the skins of hedgehogs so as to raise up a nap which was then sheared off with great scissors, leaving a smooth surface. The soft fluff so cut off was carefully

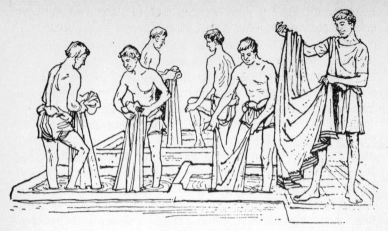

29 Fullers at work

collected and used to stuff pillows or cushions. The final operation was to sprinkle the finished cloth with water. A common practice was for fullers to fill their mouths with water and to spurt it over the cloth. Pipe-clay was also used to enhance the whiteness of the garments. Then, after a final pressing, the piece of cloth would be ready for the customer.

In this way the raw material for almost all Roman clothes was provided. Linen cloth was also made from flax, but rarely in the homes. A guild of linen-weavers, *lintones*, existed in the early days of the Republic. As Rome expanded to become a wealthy world-Empire, more linen was probably used and the domestic supply which was not always of very high quality was supplemented, as Cicero testifies, by linen imported from Egypt. Cotton was also known from an early period. It is mentioned already about 200 B.C. but although it came into general use, it was mainly for such things as great awnings and the sails of ships. The long-staple Egyptian cotton was already known in the early Roman Empire, for Pliny in his *Natural History* written in the first century A.D. said that it was softer, whiter and more fleecy than any other. Silk was little used in Republican days, and its uses did not spread during the Empire without exciting frowns. It was very expensive, because it came from the Far East and had to be paid for with gold. In the third century A.D. three pounds of gold had to be paid for one pound of raw silk dyed purple. Roman modesty disapproved of any thin clothing as transparent as silk, which was also thought degradingly effeminate for men and, what was worse, it was associated with dissolute women.

The colour of the material made up into clothes for men was almost uniformly white, as it was for most women also, although they were more free to use colours provided that they were not too garish. The Romans had a rich range of colour available from vegetable and mineral sources. Their famous purple dye came from a shell-fish, the murex. Where colour was permissible for men it was mainly in the purple bands distinguishing senators, consuls and emperors. The same purple bands but in a narrower stripe also appeared on boys' tunics until they came of age. They ran from each shoulder to the bottom of the tunic. Women had more scope. The flame-coloured bridal veil was traditional and of great antiquity, but very early in the history of the Republic women were already appearing in coloured clothes. The woollen cloth itself was not dyed but the wool was dyed in the fleece, linen, cotton and silk were dyed in the thread.

Making Roman clothes was also a simple operation. The main undergarment for all ages and sexes was a simple shift, chemise or tunic, with or without sleeves. It also seems to have served as a nightshirt or nightdress. Tunics for men and boys reached down a little below the knees. Girls' and women's tunics, *stolae*, reached to their feet and seem often to have been very gracefully pleated. Roman sewing and stitching was not very elegant. Their needles were not of fine steel as ours are today but of bone or bronze. Clumsy needles and heavy thread led to coarse stitching. It could not have been very easy to make a good buttonhole, so it is not surprising that the Romans made more use than we do of large safety pins or *fibulae* as fastenings(*11*). They had, however, buttons and studs also, but there was less scope for their use. Tunics needed merely a belt and togas were not fastened at all.

The main heavier garments, the celebrated Roman *toga* of the men and the *palla* or mantle of the women were in fact nothing more than large white blankets wrapped round the body, rather like a Highland plaid. In this primitive form they began with the early history of the Republic and so they

30 Full Roman dress

remained practically unaltered throughout almost all the thousand years of Rome's history. The toga was the badge of Roman citizenship. No marked change in fashion became noticeable until the Roman Empire was approaching its decline in the third and fourth centuries A.D. Then the men's toga tended to become larger and longer and more elaborate, while the women's long skirt-like *stola* and the mantle or *palla* which she wore over it like a large shawl tended to become shorter and smaller. The change in style in men's dress was more marked than in that of women. The toga tended to be regarded more and more as somewhat formal attire, but it never became as obsolete as a man's frock-coat for general wear has become today. Roman sculpture, particularly the pictorial reliefs on triumphal arches and on tombs and memorials (*30*), together with a review of the scanty remains of Roman painting, are almost the sole sources of reliable information on the subject. These sources are not always clear and conclusive. We know, for example, from some literary references, that women might have a hem in the shape of a coloured band or possibly a sewn-on flounce of about two inches at the bottom of the skirt of their long *stola*, but there is no pictorial evidence of what it looked like. It was a badge of modesty. Such variety as women were able to achieve in their appearance had to be sought not in the shape but in the texture, colour and decoration of their clothes. Within these narrow limits, rich women spent vast sums. Women who wanted to cut a figure at the Games or theatres were able to hire clothes for the occasion. It is remarkable that the satirist Juvenal, in one of the most bitter attacks on women ever written, has next to nothing to say about their extravagance on clothes, although he mentions jewellery and perfumes and their many other extravagances. There were no annual fashions, no special styles for spring, summer, autumn and winter, and consequently none of that tremendous investment in and publicity about women's clothing which characterises our times. In very early times women are thought also to have worn togas so that apart from their longer tunic or *stola* their dress was then basically the same as a man's as it was in the Scottish Highlands in earlier times. In the historical period, however, none but abandoned and licentious women wore togas.

Soldiers of course had helmets, but neither men nor women wore hats unless they were in the country where workers and slaves regularly wore them. Women, however, were expected to cover their heads with their mantles when out of doors, and there is a story of a sour old-fashioned Roman in Republican times who divorced his wife because she had been seen in public with her head uncovered. Her beauty, he said, was for him to see and not for the world at large.

Within limits, which must seem very narrow to us, the Romans had a keen eye for any divergencies from established styles of dress. A man whose tunic was a shade too long, a woman whose *stola* was a shade too short would find themselves the object of severe criticism. The cumbrous toga became irksome. Part of Martial's idea of happiness was to shed it: 'O! rest in tunic clad'. Such was the bliss of escaping from Rome into the country. But in Rome, to wear anything but the national dress was a serious offence. As late as A.D. 397 the Emperor Honorius proclaimed severe penalties against any man who dare appear 'in the venerable City' of Rome in trousers. Trousers were the badge of the barbarian, although knee breeches had always been regulation wear for mounted soldiers, the *equites*, when on a campaign, probably because breeches are more practical on horseback. There are not many references to Roman underclothing, but a loin-cloth or something in the nature of modern pants was also worn, otherwise, men working without a tunic, as the fullers did (29), would have offended Roman ideas of modesty. To wear nothing but a loin-cloth under a loose tunic, with a large woolly

73

blanket draped over you, is to cut clothing almost to a minimum. In the genial Italian climate this slender equipment might suffice, except in a cold winter; then the remedy against cold was to wear more tunics and a thick cloak over the toga. The first Emperor, Augustus, is said to have felt the cold so much that he wore four tunics at a time, as well as a cloak or two over his toga.

In bad weather outdoors the Romans had a variety of cloaks just as the Victorians had their various outer wrappings, ulsters, capes, reefers and so on. Some of these, particularly the very generally worn *paenula*, might be very thick and stiff, made from natural wool, probably like a coarser variety of the modern Austrian waterproof *loden* cloth. Men much exposed to the

elements, such as labourers and hunters, might have their cloaks, *paenulae*, made from leather. Such heavy outer garments were too ponderous for any pin fastening, so they had to be tied on with stout string or thongs rather as our duffle-coat was. Some may have been made in one piece with merely a hole for the head to come through. Among the many variants upon the ordinary cloak was a short cape with a hood attached, the *cucullus*. As this close-fitting cape had no sleeves it could not be worn by soldiers who had their *sagum* and, if they were centurions, their *paenulae* instead to serve them as a blanket by night. A more elegant and ornate version of this cloak was the *paludamentum* (*31*), which could only be worn by generals. The thick double circular blanket of wool long worn as a cape, called the *laena*, seems to have gone out of general use by the early Empire. The younger generation preferred the lighter hooded cloak or *lacerna*. This was also circular with a straight edge along the bottom. The two sides of it were pinned together on the right shoulder. At

31 Military dress

first it was frowned upon as undignified

for city wear. At the end of the Republic Cicero condemned Mark Antony for wearing a *lacerna* instead of a toga over his tunic. As time went on it became more widely worn and might be brightly coloured.

Clothing was expensive because it took so long to make. A present of a woollen tunic, toga or cloak could be a handsome gift particularly to impoverished hangers-on or clients of the well-to-do. 'A toga only three or four times washed', said Martial, was 'a considerable gift.' In such circumstances none but the rich had lavish wardrobes, and impoverished Romans like the poet Martial were lucky to have one good toga and a good cloak. As soon as a Roman got back home he laid aside his toga and wore only the belted tunic, except for festive occasions. Then he might put on a more sophisticated light coloured robe worn at elegant dinner parties, the *synthesis*. Like our evening dress, it was not in everybody's possession. Martial had but one, so he was rather caustic at the expense of his rich friend Zolius who made excuses to change his *synthesis* eleven times during a dinner party in order to display the rich resources of his wardrobe. At the annual great feast of the Saturnalia it was very bad manners to appear outdoors in a toga so those who had their *synthesis* usually wore it for the festival.

Children wore smaller versions of the clothes worn by their fathers and mothers(*30*). Most little boys probably wore nothing but tunics, with cloaks for bad weather (*16*). Some of the well-to-do wore small togas with a small purple band round the seam, the *toga praetexta*. Sons of humbler citizens might wear white togas but later on during the Empire, when earlier customs were less strictly observed, they seem to have adopted the *toga praetexta* also. When boyhood ceased at the age of 16 this toga of childhood would be laid aside and with it the *bulla* or lucky charm which all boys had hanging round their necks. Then the toga of manhood would be assumed, an event marked in the better families with some ceremony (p. 128).

Some little girls might possibly have worn a toga also in earlier times, since it is believed to have been worn by men and women alike in the very early days of Rome. From the scanty evidence, however, it seems unlikely that little girls were made to keep up a custom which their mothers had long abandoned, so their usual dress would have been a long *stola* or tunic reaching to the ankles, just like that of their mothers, tied round their waist or somewhat above. Over it they wore an apron-like mantle or blouse, hanging loosely and not drawn in by the belt round their stola. However, all use of the toga was not discarded, for when a girl of a well-to-do family became a young woman she, like her brother, had a ceremony at which her dolls and the clothes of childhood were laid aside and with them a toga might be included.

The relatively minor changes which are all we can detect in Roman clothing over the thousand years of the history of the Kingdom, the Republic and the Empire are another illustration of that tenacity of tradition and lack of technical development which comes out in many other aspects of everyday life in Ancient Rome.

MEALS, FOOD AND DRINK

Stories of lavish Roman banquets with exotic foods such as peacocks, ostriches, mice cooked in honey, or hundreds of larks' tongues tend to stick in the memory, giving a false impression of the eating habits of the middle-class and poorer Roman family.

In early times, Romans of all classes lived simply and economically. A tight-fisted Roman like the Elder Cato, who fed his slaves cheaply, was economical himself. He ate little meat and much uncooked food, so as to save fuel. The poorer classes of free Romans probably had rather more variety than the slaves of comparatively well-to-do people such as Cato, but their meals were rarely exciting. Religious festivals at which animals were sacrificed were the main opportunities which some of them would get to eat much meat. Special occasions, such as a birthday, a wedding, the award of a civic honour or the arrival of friends or relations, would also be celebrated if possible by a more lavish meal.

But poor as the diet of many Romans always was, they were conscious of having made great progress, for the legend was universally believed that, before the goddess Ceres came to their aid, men had to live on acorns and other wild berries. This story was no mere figment of the imagination for it has been said that the human race as a whole has eaten more acorns than it has wheat. Grateful as the Romans were expected to be to Ceres for having taught them to plough (as Virgil records) when the supplies of acorns were no longer sufficient, they looked to her in historical times for a more ample diet.

Wheat was the staple food of the great majority of Romans, whose main worry was to get enough of it. Like the Greeks before them they mostly ate it boiled as a kind of porridge. The monotony of so simple a diet was relieved by adding as many flavourings or relishes as opportunity allowed. Variety was sought by using vegetables, herbs, olives, mushrooms, fish, wild birds, and a little meat if it could be had. No doubt a skilful cook was then able to make a tasty dish out of the wheat porridge, but most cooks were slaves and their talent was mediocre, so that Roman meals were very often poor and dull. Martial says of a cook: 'I would not have his palate that of a slave, a cook ought to have his master's taste.'

Those without a staff of slaves who could nevertheless afford to hire a cook were able to do so easily enough or to get a meal from a caterer: 'say how many and at what cost you want to dine and do not add another word: your dinner is ready for you', says Martial.

Not all Romans began their day with breakfast, but those who did had a light meal, *jentaculum*, at sunrise or the first hour. 'Get up,' said Martial, 'already the baker is selling boys their breakfast, and the crested fowls of dawn are crowing all around.' School children might have a little wheat pancake biscuit or bread which their elders would also take with a little salt, honey, dates or olives. Some dipped it in wine which may be why some people dip their morning rolls in coffee in France or Italy today. A heavier breakfast with cheese or meat was unusual. The main meal, *cena*, was taken at around the ninth or tenth hour (about 2.30 p.m. to 3.30 p.m. in summer and 1.30 p.m. to 2.30 p.m. in winter) when the day's work was finished. Then the bowl of savoury wheatmeal porridge would be the main meal for most Romans, unless a more ceremonious dinner was planned or unless they were well-to-do and had no need to economise over food. Then the story was very different. A fashionable dinner party began with a great variety of the equivalent of our *hors d'œuvres*: salads, radishes, mushrooms, eggs, oysters, sardines. Romans called it the *gustatio* or *promulsio*

77

because it was followed by a drink of *mulsum* or wine sweetened with honey. Then followed the main dishes of the *cena* of anything up to six or seven courses. For this a rich variety of fish, poultry and meat was available. There were all sorts of Mediterranean fish, mackerel, tunny, mullet, eels as well as prawns, oysters and other shell-fish. Fresh-water fish was less popular among the rich, but it was to be had from the rivers and lakes while the wealthier had their private fish ponds. These would often be merely ornamental; Cicero complained bitterly that at a time when the fundamental liberties of the Roman people were at stake, the aristocrats of Rome's governing class had neither the will nor the energy to oppose Julius Caesar, because, he said, 'our leading men think themselves in the seventh heaven if they have bearded mullets in their fish ponds that will come to hand for food'. His scorn of the 'fish-breeders' was deep and merited. Meat dishes included boar, venison, wild goat, mutton, lamb, kid, sucking pig, hare and dormice. Poultry dishes were of almost every known bird: chicken, geese, ostriches, cranes, duck, partridges, pheasants, pigeons, doves, thrushes, fig-peckers, and—for the rich—peacocks. After the *cena* there was, in the old Roman tradition, a short silence while an offering of wheat, salt and wine was made to the household gods on the family altar. Then came dessert, called 'second tables'(*63*), in which every kind of honey-sweetened cakes and fruit was served. Meanwhile wines were being served by obsequious, silent slaves. This lavish personal service by a small army of sternly drilled slaves would astonish and probably embarrass us if we could experience it today. Every conceivable need or whim of any of the diners had instant attention. Flies were kept off the food by a fan, sometimes made of peacock's feathers: 'this which forbids foul flies to taste your food was the proud tail of a peerless bird', as Martial described such a fan. Romans often heated their wines and always mixed them with water. In summer the very rich would often cool their wines with elaborately preserved snow and ice. A fashionable dinner party was always prolonged after the meal was over by a long drinking session. Hours were spent drinking and talking. Mixed wine and water was brought in by slaves in a large bowl, *crater*, and from it wine was served to each guest, who had then to drink at the orders of the elected 'king of the feast'. The long evening would often be diversified by music, song, dancing girls, conjurors, dwarfs and acrobats according to the taste or the lack of taste of the host. Such long meals and floods of wine taken after a day almost without food, while lying propped up on one elbow on a long couch in a stuffy room close to a similarly reclining neighbour, perhaps of the opposite sex, were often too much of a strain for many of the guests.

Most Romans had their simple meal without guests and in the olden times they took it early so that they sometimes needed a light supper, *vesperna*, before retiring to their couches for the night, as they mostly did soon after sunset, for as we have seen, the dim light of one or two small oil lamps offered no encouragement to most of them to try to prolong the day into the night. Already by the second century B.C., the hour for the main meal got pushed back later in the day to the tenth hour between about 3 p.m. and 4 p.m. in summer and then the *cena* made the

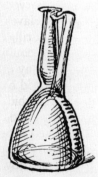

32 Glassware

vesperna superfluous. When the custom of going to a public bath each day became the habit at the end of the Republic and during the early Empire, dinner was taken after the bath, which was usually around the eighth hour. Then the habit of lunching around the sixth hour (about 11 a.m. in our time) became the rule. We know that it was fairly early because Cicero jested that 'nobody lunched during the consulship of C. Caninius Rebilus', one of Caesar's creatures, who was appointed to the consular dignity on midday, or the seventh hour, of 31 December 45 B.C., and who held power therefore for a matter of twelve hours only, for the incoming Consul for the new year took up his duties on January 1st. During the Empire, lunch, *prandium*, was a lighter meal than dinner. It could be anything from bread and cheese with a little meat eaten as a snack, like the sandwich lunch today, up to a more formal meal with hot or cold fish, poultry and meat accompanied by hot wine and water and *mulsum*.

From the first century B.C. onwards many of the wealthier Romans seemed to have become the slaves of their stomachs. Seneca, in the middle of the first century A.D., went so far as to accuse his countrymen 'of eating till they vomit and of vomiting in order to eat more'. Such was the ways of some of the rich, who naturally infected the rest of Roman society, all of whom wanted to be rich too. So the unbridled luxury of the few was a source of grievance and frustration to the many, who, for all their scorn of wealth and vice, seem, like some critics of the rich in other ages, to have been only too eager to follow their example, and to have become angry and offensive when their appetites were unsatisfied. But while the less restrained and cultivated among the very rich were 'digging their graves with their teeth', the great majority, from necessity as much as by choice, probably led a fairly healthy life on a saner and simpler diet. The fact that they mainly ate wholewheat and vegetables would go a long way towards providing that balanced diet which science has only recently discovered to be essential for proper nourishment and health.

KITCHENS AND COOKING

If a Roman said 'Come into the kitchen', what should we be likely to see? A rough idea of a Roman kitchen(*33*) can be imagined from what has been uncovered in Pompeii where hearths, pots and pans and the cooks were suddenly overtaken by the rain of ashes in A.D. 79. Most kitchens were small and simple. The fire, usually of charcoal, for the Romans had no coal, burned on a raised brick hearth and the pots and pans, very much like their modern equivalents, stood on tripods and gridirons over the hot ashes. Those who could not afford to buy charcoal had to use wood, although

33 A Roman kitchen

the smoke must have been unpleasantly strong. Houses and apartments had no proper chimneys but at most holes in the wall; larger houses had the equivalent of a chimney in the open roof, which was called the *atrium*, the 'black part'. In early times this let out the smoke and let in the rain to be collected in a pool below. But later in the Republic and Empire the *atrium* became the main sitting-room and the hearth was transferred to a kitchen.

The simple equipment found on the hearths at Pompeii would serve only for frying or boiling. To bake or to roast, an oven would be necessary and small, square or round, brick ovens were built on the hearths. When the hot fire lit inside them had reached the right temperature, the ashes would be either raked out or allowed to die down a little, and the food to be baked or roasted would be put inside and the oven door closed. A small portable version of such an oven could be used for keeping food hot in the dining-room. Elaborate bronze vessels filled with boiling water served a similar purpose. Metal cooking pots and pans(34) were rather expensive and much cooking was done in earthenware pots. They must have got stale and dirty and were easily broken, but they were cheap to buy.

Not very much has been preserved to throw light upon the very essential daily enterprise of providing food for the family and for friends. One or two Roman writers record menus or refer to meals, and something can be gleaned from them about what was cooked and served at Roman dinner parties by the host of attendant slaves.

Fortunately a compilation of cookery recipes has survived which had been collected together towards the end of the Roman Empire under the title *The Art of Cookery*, credited by the compiler to a notable gourmand whom the satirist Juvenal called 'poor niggardly Apicius', which was a remarkable effort at irony if Seneca's story about him is correct. Finding that he had spent a colossal fortune of 100 million sesterces mainly on eating and drinking and that he had only 10 million left, Apicius committed suicide. Juvenal or Martial would have regarded the annual interest alone on half a million as great affluence. The recipes collected under his name bore little relation to his own kitchen for they seem to have been compiled mainly as a guide to middle- and lower-class households, although a few more ambitious recipes are thrown in for the wealthy. An excellent English edition of it appeared in 1958, the work of two ladies, Barbara Flower and Elisabeth Rosenbaum, who not merely translated it, but tried out many of the recipes themselves. There is also a good French translation. Anyone can therefore get a good first-hand knowledge of some of the essentials of Roman cooking from these editions. There were many such Roman cookery books and they were often rewritten and, it seems, sometimes illustrated. What remain of Apicius is not complete. It does not, for instance, deal with breadmaking or with the porridge made from boiled grains, neither is it very strong on sweets.

One or two recipes for the traditional boiled wheat porridge were given much earlier by Cato the Censor in the middle of the second century B.C. 'Take half a pound of wheat, wash it well, thoroughly rub off the husk and rinse it. Then put it in a pot and cook it well. When it is done add milk by degrees until it is a

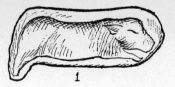

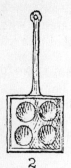

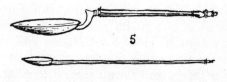

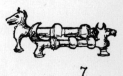

34 Kitchen utensils

1 Pastry-mould	2 Baking-pan	3 Frying-pan
4 Water heater	5 Spoons 6 Knives	7 Fire-dogs

thick porridge.' For a more tasty dish he advised adding to a pound of boiled wheat grains 'three pounds of new cheese, half a pound of honey and an egg'. This should have provided a substantial meal for several people.

The cookery book of Apicius deals with popular sauces and flavourings; with methods of preserving meat, fruit and olives; with sausages and minced meats; with vegetables; with mixed dishes of vegetables, fishes, poultry and meat; with soups and pulses (pease, beans, lentils); with poultry; with meat and with fish. A separate section was given to the special dishes beloved by more fastidious and wealthier Romans. One of Cicero's favourite dishes was the flesh of any large salt fish cooked in oil, filleted and mixed with brains, poultry liver, hard-boiled eggs and cheese, all cooked over a slow fire after being sprinkled with a sauce of pounded pepper, lovage, majoram, rue-berries, honey and oil. 'Bind it with raw eggs and garnish it with finely ground cumin seed', advised Apicius.

As is already evident from the plays of Plautus, the Romans set great store by sauces and flavourings. A cook hired in the market to cook a dinner boasts that he does not, like other cooks, 'when they cook dinners, garnish them with seasonings that eat out the bowels of the guests . . . heaping up herbs dreadful merely to mention, let alone to eat, herbs which cattle will not touch'. Pliny, writing two hundred years later than Plautus, lists scores of herbs and flavourings. The most skilful cooks probably avoided overdoing the use of strong flavourings, but there seems equally little doubt that the general practice was to disguise most natural flavours with a rich assortment of herbs, spices, nuts, honey, and wine. Sauces were thickened with a cornflour made from very finely ground wheat. Some standard sauces or relishes were in constant use, and none more so than *garum* or *liquamen*, the piquant, salty fluid made from fish or fish waste and brine. One way of preparing it was to gut tunny fish and to put the entrails and other fish waste into a vessel filled with brine and to leave it for six weeks or so. Anchovies, sprats, mackerel and other fishes were also used. Another greatly prized flavouring came from a plant called *silphium* or *laserpitium* which has never been satisfactorily identified. It has been suggested that it was assafoetida.

Concentrated wine was another stand-by in the Roman

kitchen. It was prepared by boiling wine down to about one third of its volume; the concentrated liquid known as *defrutum* was then stored for future use which appears to have been very regular. The sweeter, more syrupy mixture of honey and boiled wine was *mulsum* which has already been mentioned. This was used as a drink and not for cooking.

Not merely were such highly flavoured and spiced sauces liberally used in preparing a very wide variety of dishes, but honey also was added to dishes such as roast meat, a practice which, the English editresses of Apicius report, brings out the flavour. Even boiled eggs were to be

35 Bronze urn

eaten with a sauce compounded out of soaked pine-kernels, pepper, lovage, honey and vinegar with some of the inevitable *liquamen* or fish sauce. Strange also is another suggestion that quinces and leeks should be stewed in honey, fish sauce and concentrated wine, yet this also was tried and pronounced excellent in taste by the English editresses. The recipes contain no mention of sugar, although cane sugar was known in Rome before this cookery book was compiled. Pliny called it 'a kind of honey which collects in reeds, white like gum', adding 'it is only used in medicine'. He said that it came from Arabia, but the best was from India. For sweetening the Romans relied on honey. Dried raisins and concentrated wine and 'must', from which most of the juice of the grapes had been squeezed, were also used.

Many of the recipes are a food-reformer's nightmare and a tribute to what a good human digestive system can stand. Innocent of any notions about the science of food values, the Romans had nothing but natural instinct or ingenuity as their guide and it seems to have led them to strange lengths. Many Romans probably skipped the more ambitious sauces and concentrated upon plainer ways of cooking simpler foods, kid, lamb, veal, beef.

In earlier times, if baked bread was wanted it would first be necessary to grind grains of wheat into flour at home. It was a laborious daily job, as it still is in many parts of the world. From time immemorial until well into the historic days of the Roman Republic, the women of the household had to grind out flour. They did it very simply, by spreading wheat grains on a large flat or slightly concave stone and rubbing them over with a smaller stone which might either be round, or long and narrow like a roller. This hand-worked 'thrusting mill', as the Romans called it, survived practically up to the Christian era together with the pestle and mortar, which, however, the Romans do not seem to have used very generally until the middle of the second century B.C. But by the second century A.D. these more primitive methods of grinding had been mostly replaced by the rotary mill, *mola versatilis*, or quern. The small hand-mill or quern worked on the same principle as the Victorian hand-operated coffee-grinder. A stone in the form of a hollow cone fitted like a cap over a solid cone-shaped stone. Grain was poured in through a hole in the top stone which was revolved, so grinding the grain on the sides of the lower stone from which flour and husks fell on to a table or board.

During the later Republic and throughout the Empire most middle- and lower-class Romans relied upon commercial bakeries for their bread(55). This seems evident from what has been discovered in the provincial town of Pompeii where already by A.D. 79 there is little evidence of domestic bread making. The poorer citizens, who would have had to grind their own corn, preferred wheatmeal porridge or groats to bread: porridge meal did not need grinding and would not take so long to cook. The Romans developed a considerable discrimination, for they found out that some wheats were best for flour, bread and pastry and others better for porridge. The hulled or bearded wheat made the best porridge, as the grain was harder yet the skin of the kernel was thinner than that of the softer naked wheat.

WINE

Romans of refined taste laid great store by vintage wines. The poet Horace, a *bon-viveur* with a discriminating palate, refers with affection to a choice bottle with which he consoled himself for growing older and for the absence of the gay girls who had enlivened his earlier years. He vaunted the power of wine to chase away gloom and sadness, to inspire calm courage, to heighten the joys of friendship, to celebrate Rome's triumphs and his own deliverance from peril. It is difficult to imagine any Roman of the old school with his degree of urbanity, *savoir-faire*, yet detachment and almost nonchalance in relation to the great affairs of State. He had been a Government clerk but, like Charles Lamb very much later, he really lived only when he escaped from his ledgers into the wider world of literature and congenial friendship.

Wine drinking had not been the regular Roman habit in the earlier Republic that it became during the Empire. In earlier times Romans had been content with water and home-made brews concocted out of all manner of fruits, flowers and vegetables: figs, medlars, roses, parsley, saffron, and other strong flavourings mixed sometimes no doubt with the juice of the grape. Italy had always been known by the Greeks as a wine-producing land. The native vintages, however, were not at first valued very highly. When Julius Caesar gave a great feast in his third Consulship (46 B.C.) with four kinds of wine, two of them were Greek. Romans soon gave up their old ideas that wine was a luxury seldom to be indulged in and that no wine except Greek wine was worth drinking. One at least of the Roman vintages had long been renowned, that harvested when Lucius Opimius was Consul in 121 B.C., the year in which Gaius Gracchus was murdered. Unprecedently good weather had produced wine of quite exceptional quality, which had been stored and hoarded with such miserly care that some of it was still in existence in Pliny's day, although

36 Earthenware jars for storing wine and oil

it had by then become undrinkable. Wine drinking as one of the arts of life began to become more general from about the middle of the first century B.C. As a drink it was already quite common, for Cato in his book on agriculture and estate management allowed his slaves a pint of mixed wine and water a day. It was of course wine of the poorest quality. The relative novelty of wine-drinking in Rome is best attested by the strictness with which women were long forbidden to touch it unless it had been very heavily diluted.

Like many other strict rules of the great days of the Roman Republic, it did not survive long into the days of the Empire. The tenacity of this ancient restriction is no more surprising than the similar social conventions in England and America that kept ladies away from pubs or saloons and made it unthinkable that they should ever smoke—two social rules that were still quite strong up to the beginning of the first World War in A.D. 1914. So in Rome, women began to have the same freedom as men during the early Empire.

By Pliny's time a tremendous lore about wines had been built up, for he said that there were nearly 200 varieties; about 80 of which were of high quality; two thirds of these 'noble' wines being produced in Italy. Wines from the Greek islands, particularly the Chian, were much prized. In Rome a wine from Setia on the hills above Forum Appii was of great renown. It was the favourite wine of Augustus despite the general impression, which Horace confirms, that Caecubum wine was then the best. But its quality was not maintained because the limited area on which it was raised had been cut up when Nero began his canal from Baiae to Ostia. Falernian, another choice wine, was also grown on the favoured Campanian soil. There were several varieties of it, thin, sweet and rough, depending very largely upon the weather in the growing period. It was best when between 10 and 20 years old. There was much learned opinion about the effect of the various wines on health and digestion and much dispute about the merits of other wines, such as the Albanum and the Mamertinum. Well might Pliny sagely remark, after his long study of the subject, that 'vineyards as well as States have their rise, glory and their fall'.

The number of Romans who savoured and enjoyed wines in their pure state as connoisseurs do today seems to have been relatively small. The general practice was to mix water with wine. That it was regarded as almost essential to dilute it in this way can be seen from Horace's account of his journey to Brundisium from Rome when, at Forum Appii, he preferred to drink nothing rather than to drink the excellent Setian wine undiluted or to risk diluting it with the notoriously bad local water. Romans had other ways of doctoring wines. Mixing honey and wine was a very common practice. The *mulsum* which resulted

37 Small wine-table

was served with the first course of a Roman dinner or banquet. To make *mulsum*, according to Columella, you mixed ten pounds of honey with about three gallons (13 litres) of must, which is what remained of the grapes after they had been trodden to squeeze out the wine, but it had to be taken before it had been too much trodden. Pliny recommended using dry wine instead of must. *Mulsum* was drunk where we might now drink sherry before lunch or dinner, although the Romans drank it with their first course. It was supposed to have the great merit of whetting the appetite, aiding the digestion and promoting long life. Columella (Book XI) gives many recipes for wine.

HEALTH AND HYGIENE

Many Romans succeeded in becoming very wealthy, but not always healthy and wise. The majority of them in matters of health had no better resource than the old saying that a man is either a fool or a physician by the time he is 40; that is to say, everyone has to discover their own weaknesses and how to treat them. Great numbers of Romans, perhaps the majority, never reached the age of 40 because epidemics and diseases, combined with dirt, flies, and unhygienic food and drink, carried them off at an earlier age. There are, to be sure, stories of Romans living to an advanced age, but the evidence of tomb-stones shows that a great number died young. In the absence of statistics, it is not possible to guess the average expectation of life of a Roman at birth. Today, it is around 30 years of life for the average Indian, but nearer 70 years for the infant New Zealander. We have no reason to believe that the average Roman would have been likely to live much longer than the average Indian child today.

The physical conditions of life during the Roman Empire, poor as they would seem by our standards, were nevertheless better than those of the early Republic or of any other large communities in the ancient world. There was a lavish supply of pure water for every inhabitant; far greater than many modern cities can boast; and a reasonable system of drainage for some areas at least of the City, although the vast flood of sewage and garbage swept into the Tiber must have made life unpleasant for the bargees and riverside workers and residents, especially in the summer months. Everyone who was able to do so escaped from Rome at that time and in the early autumn, the season of fevers.

Most Romans had sufficient clothes and a roof over their heads and many were able to afford some warmth in the short but sharp winter months. As we shall see, the very poor were able to join everyone else at the Great Baths which were so magnificent a feature of the Imperial City. Physical cleanliness was therefore within the reach of the poorest Roman. Some could not go to the Baths because of ill health, and some because they were slaves chained to their toil. Soap, unknown in the Republic, does not seem to have been used as it is today. Both Martial and Pliny speak of it as 'an invention of the Gauls for giving a reddish tint to the hair'. Pliny recommended it as a remedy against scrofulous sores. He said it was made from tallow (goat's fat) and ashes and was either solid or liquid. It seems to have been expensive. In A.D. 300 a pound of soap cost two days' wages of a skilled craftsman. Other cleaning materials, such as sodium carbonate, cost twice as much.

Food, for the average Roman, was probably healthy as well as simple. The rich were just as likely to ruin their health by grossly overeating as the poor were liable to come to harm by short-commons or by bad food. The risk of infection from polluted food or water, from flies and mosquitoes and from animals and human beings smitten with diseases, afflicted rich and poor alike. The rich then, as now, were at the mercy of their cooks and washers-up whose cleanliness could not always be guaranteed.

Apart from infections, there were the usual chances and changes of life, accidents, malformations, indigestion, rheumatism, gout and all the other maladies to which the human flesh is heir. Of man-made hazards, the tremendous physical toil of the working-classes was perhaps the greatest.

The harsh labour at the grinding-mills(49), and the lack of mechanical aids in lifting and carrying, caused the strained muscles, prematurely aged hearts and physique of the toiling masses: the porters, carriers, drovers, stevedores, and particularly the carpenters.

Inside the City, the numerous little fullers' shops(29) with their crude methods and cruder chemicals must have been unhealthy as well as unpleasant. The millers' and bakers' shops need not have been so horrible as many of them were through the unnecessary dirt and neglect of their human and animal workers. Beneath the gold and the glitter of the palaces, temples and magnificent public buildings there were festering sores to discredit the boasted civilisation and urbanity of Imperial Rome —evils that were all the worse because they could have been very much reduced, yet nobody cared.

DEATH AND BURIAL

When the inevitable hour came and the family circle was broken by death, pious observances of ancient ways required that the dying should be laid upon the ground to die in contact with the earth into which they were soon to pass. Their last dying breath was caught by the nearest relative who closed the eyes of the departed, and perhaps placed a coin in his or her mouth to pay the fee of Charon, that mythical ferryman who was supposed to take them across the river Styx in the underworld. All members of the family were expected to stand by, mourning. Professional undertakers prepared the body for burial. If the dead man had held high office, he was dressed in his official robes and crowned with oak or laurel leaves which were sometimes in gold. Ordinary citizens were clad in a toga. The body lay in state in the *atrium* of the house and was attended by hired mourners. Outdoors a cypress warned passers-by that there had been a death within.

38 Part of a funeral procession

The funeral procession(*38*) might be very elaborate if the deceased was a person of distinction or very rich. The litter on which the body reclined in a life-like pose would be borne by eight men preceded by flute players for those who died young, and trumpeters for the aged, and followed by members of his family. During the Republic some men of the family would wear the life-like death-masks of their distinguished ancestors. Such a procession made a formidable impact upon the on-lookers, who would have been invited by a public crier to attend. It was on these occasions that the great men of Rome's historic past seemed once more to live and to walk the streets, parading the mighty achievements of bygone ages for the continuing admiration and gratitude of the living. When, with the rise of one-man rule and the extinction of the old noble families, these displays grew fewer and finally ceased, Rome lost one of its most powerful links with the past as well as a great stimulus to the achievement of equally great things in the future.

The procession would halt in the *Forum Romanum* where a speech would be made, a panegyric, in praise of the dead man or woman, who would then be taken on to the prepared funeral pyre. After a relative had set it aflame and the body had been consumed, the ashes, cooled by wine or water, would be collected in an urn. The funeral ceremony was preceded by a banquet and another banquet was held in the family tomb when the urn was deposited there later. After nine days' mourning, a new ritual offering of food was made at the tomb.

Sometimes these events were conducted with a princely magnificence, particularly if the dead man had been passionately admired by the multitude, as Julius Caesar had been, or hailed as the saviour of his country, as Augustus with some justice was. But insignificant, lesser men could buy their final hour of glory also; Isidorus, a freedman, left a million sesterces for his funeral expenses in 8 B.C. He could afford to, for he had a fortune of 60 millions in addition to 4,116 slaves, 3,600 pairs of oxen and 257,000 head of other cattle. At the same time he complained in his will that he 'had suffered great losses in the Civil War'. Much of such a legacy would be spent upon gladiator shows and funeral 'games', as well as the banquet.

The ashes of distinguished Romans were placed in tombs, which were often very elaborate, along the main highways leading out of the City (39). It is difficult to imagine how cluttered up by all this monumental masonry these roads must have been. The reconstruction by the famous eighteenth-century engraver Piranesi of the tombs along the Appian Way may be very wide of reality, but it is of interest in so far as it shows what might have happened after centuries of effort by countless families to perpetuate their distinction and their pride in their family line.

Needless to say the poor were unable to afford any such ceremony, perhaps not even four slaves to carry their bier,

39 Tombs of eminent citizens

93

and they often had no tomb, but were shovelled into common pits in the public cemetery on the Esquiline Hill. It was in order to avoid such a fate that small benefit societies, clubs or associations were formed. Timid rulers fearful of conspiracies and riots allowed none but such harmless unions or societies as these, apart from traders' guilds, and their sole aim was to provide a periodical dinner reunion and to find modest funeral expenses for their members. Their urns, like the urns of the slaves and the freedmen of large families, might then find a resting place in niches in the wall of some large tomb or catacomb. Several thousand urns might be fitted into such a place. They were called dovecotes, *columbaria*(*40*), and there must have been hundreds of them.

40 *Columbaria*

Chapter IV

SLAVERY

ORIGINS AND DEVELOPMENT OF SLAVERY

THE whole style and quality of life in Ancient Rome was degraded by its dependence upon slave labour. It was the common practice in all Mediterranean lands to use human beings as though they were animals or tools, but no people in recorded history owned so many slaves or relied as heavily upon slave labour as the Romans.

Before the third century B.C. none but the very rich had large numbers of slaves. A small-scale Roman farmer managed his holding of two to five acres (0·8 to 2 hectares) helped by his family or with one or two slaves. They would probably also have been natives of Italy, folk very like himself and his wife. They helped on the farm and in the house, living as one of the family. The links in Rome between the slaves and members of the family might indeed be even closer, for many were brought into the family life and worship and shared in its religious celebrations, particularly the *Saturnalia*, the ancient mid-December feast (p. 186). No people who had such ceremonies could have entirely forgotten the common humanity which united themselves and their slaves.

So long as Rome increased her territory and power at the expense of neighbouring Italian peoples, the majority of the slaves were Italian. But in the second and first centuries B.C. the first striking change in traditional practice occurred, when hordes of foreign slaves began to pour into Rome as a result of many campaigns by Roman armies in Spain, Greece, Macedonia, Asia Minor, and later under Julius Caesar in Gaul and Britain. The Island of Delos became a wholesale market for slaves from Asia: in one day thousands of slaves might change hands there, to be shipped like cattle to Rome where they were exhibited, men, women and children, naked in the slave-markets, and sold one after the other to the highest bidder (*41*). If they had just been brought to Rome their feet were whitened with chalk and a placard was hung round their necks advertising their qualities and defects, for the market inspectors, the *aediles*, would hold the seller responsible for any false statement about their merchandise, human or otherwise. The choicest slaves were probably disposed of privately to rich customers.

Capture by war was the main source of slaves during the Republic and early Empire and it was often one motive for war. In early times army commanders were proud to bring back such handsome dividends to the public Treasury. During the last century of the Republic, this ancient honesty was set aside. Sulla, Pompey and Caesar became immensely rich after their successful campaigns by regarding much of what their troops had looted, particularly the slaves, as their own private property. Many slaves were also secured by piracy, by kidnapping even on the streets of Rome, as well as on the highways. The children of mothers who were slaves became slaves in their turn, the property of whoever owned the mother. As foreign conquests ceased during the later Empire, the children of slaves became a

41 Sale of a foreign slave

main source of supply. Some free-born children cast out by their parents might be taken up by others and reared as slaves, although it was illegal to make slaves out of the children of free-born Romans. Once enslaved, however, it would have been very difficult to rescue them. That there was a vast increase in the number of slaves in Rome after the second century B.C. is certain, but how many there were is not known. Vast numbers were sent to labour under harsh treatment in the country. Probably the Romans themselves did not know how many there were. It seems likely that throughout the last five centuries of Roman history there would have been about five to seven million people in Italy, of whom about two million were slaves. There were also about a quarter of a million free foreigners. Slaves, of course, were not shared among all families equally, but anyone, even another slave, could buy them.

COST OF SLAVES

The price of slaves varied very much. After a successful campaign they would be a glut on the market and many would be sold very cheaply. At the time of Plautus, when the value of money was greater than it became under the Empire, Cato, who always drove a hard bargain, was ready to pay from 500 to 1,500 *denarii* for a slave. He got very angry when wealthy Romans were ready to pay as much as 2,500 *denarii* for a pretty boy or girl slave and as soon as he had the power, as Censor of the Republic, he put a heavy tax on such luxuries. According to some prices mentioned by Plautus, two children and their nurse could be bought for 1,800 *denarii* while the prices of pretty girls varied from 2,000 to 6,000 *denarii*; a music girl cost 4,000 *denarii*. Two hundred years later these prices would be rather low. A skilled labourer for a vineyard in the reign of Augustus cost 2,000 *denarii*. But in fact a slave, like a picture, a marble statue, or a rare book, was worth what any rich person was prepared to pay. Towards the end of the Republic and in the early Empire some fantastic prices were recorded; Martial complained that anything from 25,000 to 50,000 *denarii* was paid for boys, and he also recorded that a low-class girl found no bidder at 150 *denarii*. Suetonius, a generation later, records that a grammarian 'Lutatius Daphnis is known to have been bought by Quintus Catulus for 175,000 *denarii* and soon afterwards set free'.

To get some idea of what these figures mean they must be compared with other costs. Cicero spent 25,000 *denarii* a year to have his son educated in good style in Athens. For his fine town house, because it had been built for the millionaire Crassus, Cicero paid 875,000 *denarii*. Many poor Romans had less to spend on buying their small house than rich people would be ready to pay for a slave; while some rich folk spent more on a single large fish for a dinner party than the price of a poor slave.

SLAVE LABOUR

Only the rich could afford many slaves and they, of course, also had the best. As many more Romans became wealthy under the Empire there was keen competition for skilled and beautiful slaves. 'The first question to be asked', said Juvenal, about any man 'will be about his wealth, the last about his character. How many slaves does he maintain? How much land does he possess? How many courses does he have served at table and how much does he provide for his guests?' The most intelligent slaves came from Greece. Clever Greeks were to be found in many rich Roman households as doctor, tutor, librarian, musician, goldsmith, artist. Romans in business in the City, who could not afford to keep so many skilled slaves for their own personal service, used them as shop-assistants or craftsmen manufacturing such things as silverware, jewellery, fake antiques, tables, tripods, sculpture and books. In addition to the skilled, well-educated slaves in the house of the well-to-do there would be very many more employed as cooks, barbers, valets, butlers, waiters, silver polishers, doormen, porters, letter carriers, furnacemen, cleaners and gardeners. The lady of the house would have her retinue of slave girls who had to obey her slightest whim. In the luxurious days at the height of the Empire some of them would be highly specialised and skilled as hairdressers, perfumers, dressmakers, ladies' maids, masseuses, manicurists and so on. When a wealthy master or mistress left the house for a journey, to pay a call or to dine with friends, whether on foot or by litter (*42*), they would be accompanied by a bodyguard of slaves. At night, the lurking thugs and gangsters did not venture to attack a wealthy man with his 'scarlet cloak and long retinue of attendants, carrying torches and brass lamps',

42 A rich lady being carried in a litter

whereas, says Juvenal, the poor man, 'escorted by the moon or by the feeble light of a candle whose wick has to be made to last', falls an easy victim to the bully's club or fists.

As all human booty captured in war was the property of the Republic, it is not surprising that a part at least of the labour force employed in the service of the City of Rome should have been slaves. There was a great deal to be done every day in a city of about a million inhabitants. The maintenance and construction of roads, bridges, aqueducts and other public buildings required the services of many men. Much constructional work was undertaken by private contractors using slave labour; maintenance work, with all its attendant clerical and accounting duties, would be more suitably undertaken by the City authorities directly. The two Consuls had publicly owned slaves to help with routine work, and other magistrates, particularly the Aediles, whose duties were to keep the City tidy and orderly and to prevent cheating in the markets, and the Quaestors, who collected taxes and acted as Treasury officials, would be in special need of workmen and clerks. One advantage of slave labour was that on any suspicion of wrong-doing they could be made to confess under torture and, as they and all they owned belonged to their masters, the risk of their embezzling public funds or property was of small importance. A slave employed in the service of the Republic or as a temple attendant enjoyed a higher status than slaves privately owned: they were, after all, officials, even if of minor grade, and they borrowed dignity from their office as minor officials often try to do. Some married free women and left a proud account of themselves on their tombstones.

Under the Empire the ranks of public slaves began to grow larger. Firm rule by one man, which almost everybody realised, however reluctantly, to be essential if government was to become a reality, could not be effective unless he had a considerable staff. Whether the Emperor wanted to make himself responsible for the public welfare of the Roman people or not, he was forced into it by the very nature of his position. He inherited from the Republic the task of ensuring an adequate corn supply; if it began to fail it was the Emperor who was blamed. 'When there was a scarcity of grain because of long continued droughts the Emperor Claudius was once stopped in the middle of the Forum by a mob', Suetonius records, 'and was so pelted with abuse and pieces of bread, that he was barely able to escape to the Palace by a back door. After this experience, he neglected no means of bringing grain to Rome even in winter.' Another essential service was the water supply. The publicly and annually elected magistrates during the Republic had, over nearly 200 years, built and maintained four aqueducts channelling fresh, pure water from the Anio and the springs of Frascati into the City(*43*). Augustus made his trusted friend Agrippa responsible for the supervision of the entire system which he undertook by using 240 of his own slaves for the work of repair. By his will he bequeathed them to Augustus, who made them over to the Senate as public slaves serving a new official Water Commissioner. Four new aqueducts had been added to those of the Republic. The Emperor Claudius added the *Aqua Claudia*, 120 miles long (193 kilometres). In all, the conduits were nearly 300 miles (483 km), about 50 miles (80 km) of which ran underground or in covered channels bringing about 40 gallons (182 litres) a day for every inhabitant in Rome. The operating staff rose to 460 slaves whom

43 An aqueduct

Claudius took into the Imperial service, setting one of his liberated slaves, a freedman, in charge of them. Rome's water supply, like the corn supply, thus became a recognised Imperial responsibility.

At the end of the first century A.D. the Emperor Nerva appointed a born administrator, Sextus Julius Frontinus, as superintendent of the system. His report is the only comprehensive survey we have of any part of the public administration of ancient Rome. It was, of course, a relatively small element in the whole complicated business of the affairs of the largest Empire Europe has ever known. The administrative work involved in keeping in touch with the commanders of the Roman Army in the field, with provincial governors and the whole army of imperial officials must have been immensely demanding in time and staff. Roads, temples, mines, quarries, the Imperial post, the Mint and the corn supply also involved much detailed administrative work and then there was the management of the Emperor's revenues upon which the whole machinery of State depended. Slave labour kept it all in motion.

The fear in which Romans lived of their slaves during the first centuries B.C. and A.D. has many illustrations. Any slave trying to pass himself off as a free citizen might be put to death. By ancient tradition none but free citizens might serve in the Roman army; any slave who enlisted in the army was liable to summary execution immediately he was discovered. Slaves were, however, made to serve behind the lines providing transport and every kind of heavy manual labour, as well as becoming clerks in the army pay service. It used to be believed that slaves were made to tug the oars in the navy, but when Augustus put 20,000 of them to do so it is said that he first made them freed men. The Romans would never put weapons into the hands of slaves so slaves would never be armed for the fray to join the free citizen-soldiers who were the backbone of the navy as a fighting force. Sea battles were decided by the number and battle-worthiness of the armed men carried on each vessel, which were less men-of-war than fast troop transports, so when the fighting got very hot it was likely that rowers might join in: their own lives were at stake.

TREATMENT OF SLAVES

The plays of Plautus (c. 251–184 B.C.) abound in references to the brutal treatment of slaves, and this was before the vast influx into Rome of oriental and foreign slaves. In one of the best of the plays a nasty character called Ballio is shown roaring at his slaves and laying about them with a heavy whip. 'Get out of it you scoundrels, bought at a loss and kept at a loss, whom I can't get to do a thing aright unless I try this way', whereupon he flogs them all round. 'Never did I see human beings more like asses, so toughened with beating that when you flog them you hurt yourself more than you hurt them. Whenever they get a chance they pilfer, purloin, pinch and plunder, eat, drink and run away, that's their line.' The plays abound with threats of scourging, lashing, flogging, breaking ankles and torture and the ever-present fear of death by crucifixion to which any slave could be condemned. In another play a slave says, 'I know that the cross will be my tomb: there are laid my forefathers, my father, grandfather, great-grandfather, great-great-grandfather'. Nevertheless most of the slaves manage to avoid a beating and a number of them contribute to the happy ending of the play by earning their freedom.

Already in these early times many Romans were not without a conscience about the miserable situation of their slaves. When a slave in another of the plays of Plautus tells his master, 'Nature produces all men free and by nature all desire freedom.

Slavery is worse than any evil, than every calamity; and he whom
Jupiter hates, he first makes a slave', the master admits 'You
speak not unwisely': words that were echoed by Cicero a
hundred years later. Yet even in Cicero's day a friend of his,
the learned Varro, could write of the three chief instruments
which the farmers had to help them: those without voice such
as waggons, those with inarticulate voices such as oxen and those
with voices, the slaves. In spite of the brutality of some masters
and mistresses, the horrors of Roman slavery were considerably
modified by the humane way in which many slaves were treated
by considerate and thoughtful masters. In times of persecution
and personal danger we know that many were loyally served
and shielded by their slaves out of gratitude and affection, and
this even at the cost of their lives. The situation in better homes
perhaps resembled domestic service in the great houses of
England and Ireland in the eighteenth and nineteenth centuries.
Although that way of life has left some grim memories of hard
work for low pay with uncomfortable quarters in attics and
basements, there is no doubt that vast numbers of 'domestics'
got more out of their hard life of monotonous service than they
could have done in any alternative employment open to them.
The security, protection, elegant surroundings, the companion-
ship of their fellow servants, and the wider interests which life
in a large household with a distinguished owner often afforded,
were positive values of no mean order. Many Roman slaves had
similar advantages, all of which, under a wealthy and kind
master, probably gave life more meaning than it had for some
free men, struggling to win a precarious livelihood on land or
sea. Some slaves might be exceptionally lucky, such as those left
in charge of one of their rich master's country or seaside villas.
Servitude then could be little different from the life of a free
caretaker. In large households there were necessarily grades of
authority and distinction among the slaves themselves, just as the
butler and the housekeeper lorded it over the servants' halls in
the days of the great houses of England, and many of the evils
of slavery came from those in posts of subordinate authority
rather than from the actual slave-owner. When slaves could look
forward to promotion to such positions of command, and when
they were in the service of trusting masters, they would have
been able to shed much of the feeling of inferiority and utter

44 Slave driving his master's coach

helplessness that slavery naturally produces. It is very evident, for example, that Cicero lavished as much thought and affection upon his trusted personal assistant and slave Tiro, as he did upon his own son or nephew. It is also difficult to believe that a slave in the Imperial Service who owned a dozen or more slaves of his own went in daily fear of life and limb as the slaves depicted by Plautus might have done.

But the essential difference between slave and free man remained. When Cicero saw his countrymen, lulled by the magic of Julius Caesar's genius, weakly surrendering their Republican liberties in the hope of enjoying the wise and beneficent rule of one man, he put before them the plain truth about the danger of absolute autocracy. At all costs, he told them, they should fight against such political servitude for it was a form of slavery. Slavery was an unthinkable fate for a free Roman because 'even if one's master be not tyrannical, yet it is a most miserable thing that he should be able to be so if he chooses'. Human societies continue to grapple with the problem of reconciling their need for that political leadership without which nothing gets done with their equal need for independent choice and action without which human energies and creative will-power atrophy and die. The Romans did not succeed in creating a State and a government which would be powerful for good yet impotent for harm.

Apart from the personal fate of the men, women and children who became slaves, the results of slavery were to be seen not only in the way of life of very rich Romans; they also influenced directly the lives of the ordinary people. Thousands of Romans

104

who might have earned a living by making shoes, clothes, furniture, jewellery, and all the thousand and one things used by the well-to-do Romans had fewer opportunities to do so because these things were made within the households of the rich by their slaves. And, what was worse, honest toil by free men was despised because it meant doing what a slave should do. Lower forms of human life were held cheaply. It is not difficult to see how this state of affairs upset the business and industrial life of Ancient Rome and blocked its development and progress. Because of slavery there was not the mass demand for everyday goods that is a feature of our times. Moreover, when slave labour was cheap and abundant there was no strong motive to invent expensive machinery. Maybe the Romans would not have been clever enough to invent any very complicated machinery, even if they had not owned so many thousands of slaves. For they would have had to find new sources of power to replace the slaves. They had some water mills, and their engines of war were powerful and ingenious, but natural sources, such as water power, limited the location of industry to a few favourable sites and when they were used, the problem of efficient transport of heavy raw materials, such as wheat, and products such as flour, became acute.

'Capitalism' therefore in Ancient Rome did not fulfil its modern function of diminishing the burden of human toil by making possible the construction of machines, so the consequent failure of the ancient world to progress in industry and technology may, in part at least, be attributed to reliance upon slave labour.

SLAVE REVOLTS

Frequent harsh punishment and the constant fear of torture, mutilation and death drove slaves to try to escape, to mutiny and to murder their oppressors. The Roman slave owners were only too well aware of such dangers and they took all the precautions they could against them. Legally a runaway slave was himself a thief. He had stolen his master's property. There were strict laws against giving him any help. In the course of time a kind of private detective agency made a business of tracking down and capturing slaves who had escaped. Augustus took credit early in his career for having returned 30,000 escaped

105

slaves to their masters 'for punishment'. A runaway slave was therefore very likely to be caught, and then his punishment might be exemplary to terrify any of his fellow slaves. If a slave murdered his master all the other slaves in the household were liable to be put to death as accomplices. In this atmosphere of hate and fear, it is not surprising that one of the ways political conspirators usually collected their forces was to promise freedom to any slaves who would fight for them. When Cicero was Consul in 63 B.C. a disappointed, ambitious aristocrat, Lucius Sergius Catilina, freed slaves to swell the motley crew of desperadoes he had recruited. Only ten years earlier, 90,000 slaves, under the leadership of a Thracian gladiator called Spartacus, had revolted and they were not finally defeated before they had inflicted fearful suffering upon their former masters, just like a victorious and savage foreign army. With disasters of such a magnitude fresh in Roman memories, it is not surprising that Catilina and his crew of cut-throats, after being denounced as enemies of the Republic, were pursued by a Roman army and defeated in a pitched battle. Memories of these horrors remained to harden many Romans against any relaxation in the harsh control of slaves. Over one hundred years later, when the prefect of Rome, Pedanius Secundus, was murdered by a slave in A.D. 61, his whole household of some 400 slaves were, according to ancient custom, condemned to die. By this time public opinion revolted against such cruelty and the matter came before the Senate where, says Tacitus, many 'pitied the number, age or sex of the victims, and the undoubted innocence of the great majority'. In spite of such protests, the execution was approved. Public indignation was so great that soldiers had to line the route along which the slaves were led to be slaughtered.

Cruel masters and mistresses were still too many. Around A.D. 60, Seneca, in a well-known letter, quoted, as though it were just as true in his day as when Cato had said it two hundred years earlier: 'You have as many enemies as you have slaves'; and the reason was, he said, 'the inhuman and cruel way we treat them, not as though they were men but as beasts'. The fact that a Stoic like Seneca, for whom it was a matter of pride to be indifferent to pleasure or pain, could make his strong protest shows that by his day some slave owners, at least, were kind and considerate. From the time of Augustus, laws had begun to limit the maltreatment of slaves. By the *Lex Petronia* in the first century A.D., for instance, no slave could be sent to fight to the death in the arena unless he had previously been judicially condemned for some crime. Claudius made it an offence to kill or abandon slaves who were ill and unfit for work. Succeeding Emperors tried to prevent slaves becoming the helpless victims of a revolting white slave traffic.

FREEDMEN AND FREEDWOMEN

The better the slaves were treated by their masters, the more expensive they were to maintain and the more therefore the slave approached the condition of the free man. When it cost as much or more to keep a slave as it did to hire a free man, it was no longer good business to maintain vast armies of slaves, unless they were needed, as they often were, for other than strictly business reasons, such as for show, or for domestic service. They would be an expensive luxury at a time when the State was giving free citizens all the wheat and water they needed for nothing. Whether such economic considerations alone prevailed, or whether the spread of a greater fellow-feeling was responsible, it seems clear that already in the first century A.D. the practice of freeing slaves (45) had become more common, despite the frightening increase in the slave population at that time. There were therefore good business reasons to help the moralists who began to doubt whether Aristotle, Cicero and Varro had been right in believing that

45 Manumission, or ceremonial freeing of a slave

107

slavery was inevitably part of the nature of things. The Stoic view began to be heard more insistently, that all men are brothers, born with equal rights, and that freedom depends on the mind or spirit and cannot be limited by accidental distinctions arising from birth or social condition.

A generous master such as Cicero would give his slaves pocket money, which they could save if they chose because they lived 'all found' and there was no need for them to spend money. Many slaves were able to buy their freedom with their own savings which a generous master would probably let them keep, to help them to get a good start in their new independent careers. Others gained their freedom as a reward for faithful service even if they had perhaps to wait until their master or mistress died, when they would be given their freedom as a legacy. Some few lucky ones were left fortunes by their masters. A large class of freedmen and freedwomen thus came into existence who were really only Roman in name. No vigorous policy of 'Romanising' them was ever adopted. They picked up the old Roman traditional values by chance instead of being drilled in the Roman way of life. Their dependence upon their former master continued to the extent that they still looked to him for advice and protection and legal help in meeting the problems and difficulties of the great world. These dependent people joined the ranks of the free 'clients' of the rich. The dependence of the former slave would be denoted by his foreign name, to which the family name of his former owner would be added. Having tasted adversity and having had to work hard and to live by their wits, many of these former slaves made good use of their freedom.

Romans of the old school did not like the rapid advancement of former slaves and many must have echoed Pliny's comment recalling how his forefathers had seen 'standing within a cage, with a mark of chalk on their feet and a lock about their heels', an infinite number who, 'all being by their masters enfranchised, became wonderfully rich by the bloodshed and goods of Roman citizens in that licentious time of proscriptions' at the end of the Republic. 'And yet', Pliny adds, 'we in our days have known the same persons to climb into the place of highest honour and authority.' Despite the uneasiness of reflective, intelligent rulers such as Augustus, who wished to limit the freeing of slaves, the

Emperors were as much responsible as anyone for this development. Imperial public officials in Rome were servants of the Emperors in a more direct, personal way than British civil servants are in the service of the reigning monarch as the head of the State. They were either the Emperor's slaves or his personal servants whom he had perhaps freed from a condition of slavery. The more able and industrious slaves were promoted and given their freedom so that Romans would not be ruled by slaves. But a freedman had always been regarded as having an inferior social status to a freeborn citizen. When such freedmen, working closely with their Imperial masters, made vast fortunes and had the first families of Rome eating out of their hands, it is no wonder that Romans of the old school became embittered. Freedmen who had risen in the Imperial Service were apt to become intoxicated by their elevation. 'They had', Pliny said, 'in their fortune grown insolent.'

The Romans themselves created these social and economic problems, which arose from the swarms of freedmen and women who thronged the City, taking over very much of the day-to-day work. In the end, the freedmen devoured their creators. By the second century A.D. it has been estimated that eight out of ten of the men, women and children who walked the streets of Rome had slave blood in their veins. The background to the lives of very many of them was alien to the old Roman tradition. They would not have felt the loss of political liberty which they and their ancestors had never known, as the terrible disaster which it was to Cicero and the old Republicans. From Asia, Africa, Egypt and Gaul, they brought strange mystery religions and new un-Roman habits and behaviour. Powerful though the traditions of old Rome undoubtedly were, a sea of new beliefs, new superstitions, new uncertainties was lapping round the moral and religious foundations of the City. Forces were at work within Rome and among the Romans themselves to change their outlook on life, and these together with the influence of the slaves and the freedmen and women slowly caused the ancient fabric of the Roman style of life to crumble away. By the second century A.D. this process had already gone far, despite a succession of good Emperors. When bad ones followed, autocracy and absolutism proved disastrous, so preparing the way to the weakness and confusion of the third century and to the collapse at the end of the fourth century.

At the end of the Empire, when the capital of the Western World had been moved to Byzantium (now Istanbul) the Emperor Justinian (A.D. 527–65) caused a summary of all the laws of Rome to be prepared in a great Digest (A.D. 530–4). References are made in it to the prices of slaves in the gold money of that time. Now Justinian was a Christian Emperor and Christianity had been a favoured religion of the Roman Empire for nearly 200 years when this Digest was published. So Christianity did not succeed in killing slavery, although it much modified and softened the habits of many slave owners.

Stoic philosophy had prepared the way for the Christian attitude. Seneca, who professed the Stoic doctrine, in an often-quoted letter to his friend Lucilius (XLVII), throws a revealing shaft of light upon Roman attitudes to slavery in the first half of the first century A.D. which he heartily condemned, proclaiming instead: ' "Live with your inferiors in just the same way as you would like your superiors to live with you." That is the very essence of my advice.'

Chapter V

EARNING A LIVING

W HEN Roman schools gave no training in handwork or in technical skills, and when there were thousands of slaves to do most of the manual work and a great deal of highly skilled work as well, there were far fewer opportunities for free Roman citizens to earn a living. After their simple rudimentary schooling, which most completed at an early age, what did the boys and girls of Ancient Rome expect to do in life?

For most girls, throughout Roman history the answer is easy: they were married. There were no jobs for them in shops, offices or in domestic service. During the Empire there are references to a few women teachers, doctors and hairdressers, but they were exceptional. Slaves or freedmen were employed for all that sort of work. A girl was often betrothed or promised in marriage while still an infant. Romantic attachments met a hard fate in the Ancient Roman tradition if parents had other plans for their sons and daughters. For a girl to remain un-married much beyond the teenage was unusual. As a young matron or housewife, in Rome's early days and for a very long time afterwards, unless she was rich, she would have to care for her home and children with such skills as she might have learned from her mother, including spinning and weaving. In any family household above the poverty-line such monotonous toil and all hard work would be undertaken by slaves.

In the early days of the Republic, for boys also there was no problem. They followed in their father's footsteps, which meant that most of them had to learn how to cultivate their patch of land, to manage the family farm or smallholding and at the same time to learn how to become good soldiers, ready to fight, and all-too-often to defend hearth and home with their lives. Yet even then not all Romans were farmers. Somebody had to build the houses, temples, bridges, and the aqueducts bringing water to the City. Someone had to kill animals, sell the meat, bake bread, and make and sell pots, cooking vessels, shoes, sandals, ploughs, grinding mills, nails, hammers, carts, waggons, saddles, bridles, scythes, rakes, hoes, swords, shields, spears, knives, axes, ropes, ladders and the hundred and one things a farming community and a fighting community would expect to be able to buy in the market place or get in time of need. From the earliest times, therefore, there was a considerable industry of the sort to be found in any small country town before the invention of machinery. Such fairly simple industries never died away, but, on the contrary, grew and expanded as Rome itself developed. For the great mass of the Roman people this mainly agricultural pattern of life provided the setting in which they had to live for many centuries. The girls got married and kept house; the boys worked on the farm, fought in the army and a few became craftsmen, shopkeepers or carriers. As Rome developed into the imperial capital of the world, this simple way of life became less significant, and Romans relied more and more upon the Italian countryside and the resources of their Empire for the basic necessities of life, and for manpower in the army as well as in industry. They were able to make others work for them.

Because the hard work, the dirty work, and nearly all the manual labour was done by slaves and by men and women who had been slaves, and because slaves were regarded as a lower form of life, all manual work was thought degrading. And not manual work alone; Cicero, in the guide to life and social duty which he wrote for his son at the end of the Republic, summed up the Roman attitude by saying: 'It is our duty to honour and reverence those who, as true patriots, have rendered or are now rendering efficient service to their country, just as much as if they were invested with some civil or military authority.' Strange to say, he did not seem to regard working for a living as being service to the country, for he at once goes on to discuss 'trades and other means of livelihood'. He wished his son to be interested only in

those suitable for a free man. Gentlemen should not soil themselves with means of livelihood which provoke ill-will, such as collecting customs dues and money-lending. Degrading and vulgar also are the gains of all hired workmen whom we pay for manual labour and not for their artistic skill, because their wages are the very

46 Carrier's waggon leaving a wine-merchant's shop

badge of servitude. All mechanics are occupied in a degrading way, for no workshop can have anything about it worthy of a free man.

Cicero took the same attitude to trade as he did to industry: 'we must also despise those who buy from wholesale merchants in order to resell immediately, for they would make no profits unless they lied abominably, and there is nothing meaner than misrepresentation'. There were evidently grades of depravity in trade, for Cicero said that 'least respectable of all are the trades catering for sensual pleasures, fishmongers, butchers, cooks, poulterers and fishermen. You can add perfumers, dancers and variety performers.' Cicero had many friends in the higher ranks of business on whom he was often dependent, so he qualifies his condemnation of them by saying that 'if trade is on a great scale, importing large cargoes from all parts of the world and distributing them to many people without misrepresentation, it is not to be so much disparaged'. However, a gentleman should get out of it as quickly as he conveniently could, for 'it even seems to deserve the greatest respect if those who have been engaged in it, satisfied with the fortunes they have made, retreat from the port to farmlands'. Then their shady past might be overlooked because 'of all the occupations by which gain is made, none is better than agriculture, none more profitable, none more delightful, none more becoming to a gentleman'.

ROME'S IMPORTS AND THEIR TRANSPORT

A very large part of the population of Rome must have suffered a social stigma from the nature of their daily work, because a city of about a million inhabitants cannot be kept going unless most of them take a hand in supplying common needs. By Cicero's day and throughout the four centuries of the Empire, Rome was no longer self-supporting. Farmlands near the City which used to supply the simple fare of the Fathers of the Republic had then long been covered with suburban villas, elegant estates of the well-to-do, roads and wayside tombs. Rome never had many industries producing articles for the export market, so the cost of the huge imports needed every day came from the tribute, taxes, rents and other exactions extorted from all the provinces which the Romans had acquired by force of arms.

Wheat was the first necessity and in the early Empire it came

mainly from Africa (10,000,000 bushels) (30·6 million dekalitres), Egypt (5,000,000) (18m. dekalitres) and Sicily (2,000,000)
(7·27 m. dekalitres). All these imports, nearly half a million tons
(over half a million tonnes), came mostly to Rome's great port
of Ostia, only about two days' sailing distance from North
Africa. Then it was trans-shipped into barges and towed by oxen
or slaves upstream to Rome. The grain barges competed for
space on the towpath with barges bringing other supplies up to
the City (47). By the second century about half the wine drunk
in Rome came from Spain, but supplies from the favoured
Campanian soil south of Rome were also shipped to Ostia. So
was a large tonnage of olive oil, mostly from Africa and Spain.

Ostia was crowded with commercial concerns and the government had a large staff supervising the corn supply whose
headquarters were in Rome. Throughout the first century A.D.,
the official corn ships had Roman soldiers on board to prevent
theft and adulteration of the precious cargo, the property of the
State. Huge warehouses lined the new Imperial harbour at Portus,
while the offices were in the old town two miles away but connected by a canal to the Port. Portus Augusti, extended by
Trajan and called also Portus Trajani, slowly sank into decay

47 A wine-laden barge being towed up the Tiber, from Ostia to Rome

with the town of Ostia after the collapse of Rome in the fifth century A.D. To reduce Rome to submission the barbarian invaders had only to capture the port with the granaries on which the City depended, as Alaric, King of the Goths, did in A.D. 409. The harbour, no longer dredged and cleared as it had been in the heyday of the Empire, was filled with silt from the Tiber and the sea receded. Sand was blown over the ruins of the deserted town. Not until recent times have any large-scale excavations been undertaken, but now much of the outline of a city, once more populous, busy and much more 'modern' than Pompeii or Herculaneum, has been revealed.

The bustle of life, the comings and goings to ship-side, inspecting and checking deliveries, loadings on barges (*48*), payments to masters, crews, bargees, lightermen, engagement of crews to replace men lost overboard or deserters, must have kept an army of clerks and overseers hard at work. The masters and crew were mostly foreigners. There was no form of insurance until Claudius, in his anxiety over supplies and to stimulate shippers to risk winter voyages, guaranteed to make good any loss suffered by storms. He also gave political privileges to encourage men and women to invest in the shipping industry.

The lightermen formed the largest guild in Ostia. The bargees with their ox teams, the corn-measurers, shipwrights, caulkers, rope-makers, divers, dock labourers, stevedores, porters,

48 Loading a barge at Ostia

warehousemen and warehouse guards, carpenters, wood merchants, oil-men, wine merchants, hide and leather dealers, all had their guilds and associations at Ostia. From what we know of their names it is evident that the great majority of their members were either slaves or former slaves.

The organisation of trade, rudimentary as it might seem in these days of fast ships, aeroplanes, radio and telegraphy, nevertheless delivered the goods. 'Whatever is raised or manufactured by each people is assuredly always here to overflowing', said Aelius Aristides in his praise of Rome around A.D. 150:

> So many merchantmen arrive here with cargoes from everywhere, at every season and with each return of the harvest, that the city seems like a common warehouse of the world. Cargoes from India, Arabia Felix, clothing from Babylonia and luxuries from the barbarian lands beyond. . . . Egypt, Sicily and the civilised parts of Africa are your farms. The arrival and departure of ships never ceases, so that it is astounding that the sea, not to mention the harbour, suffices for the merchantmen.

BUILDING

Building or rebuilding, on a vast scale, was going on in Rome all the time. Strabo said in the first century A.D. that whenever any Roman bought a house he at once began either to alter it or to pull it down and rebuild. Architects, surveyors, contractors, labourers, transport and haulage men, not all of whom would have been slaves, were kept hard at work.

There was a constant stream of barges bringing stone, brick, marble, granite and wood up the Tiber and down its tributaries, particularly the Anio. The heavier blocks and columns had to be moved through the city on rollers, and this work was done by slaves and beasts of burden.

In times of crisis, such as the rebuilding of Rome after disastrous fires or when one of the more lavish Emperors was undertaking great new buildings or restoring and repairing old ones, the traffic jams and the noise caused by heavy transport would madden the miserable citizens. By Julius Caesar's command, as we have seen, all ordinary traffic had to circulate at night. But the material needed for public buildings was allowed by day also. 'In what rented lodgings is it possible to sleep?' asks Juvenal's friend; 'the coming-and-going of carts in the narrow, winding streets and the curses of the drivers of the blocked teams rob the heaviest sleepers of rest.' No wonder he said 'it takes great wealth to sleep in the city', for then some vast villa provided bedrooms round a quiet inner courtyard or peristyle.

After the tremendous conflagration which devoured the greater part of the City in Nero's day the rubble and debris was taken down to Ostia in barges to be used in harbour construction. To replace the burnt houses, shops, temples and public buildings an immense quantity of brick, stone, marble, timber, sand and limestone was required. The cost was terrific and the whole Empire was laid under contribution. Rome had seen nothing like it before and the boasted achievements of Augustus, who said that he found a city of brick and left one of marble, were eclipsed. In the following generation, Titus completed the great amphitheatre, the Colosseum (76). About 200,000 tons (tonnes) of travertine and another 200,000 tons (tonnes) of tufa, brick and mortar were used to build it.

How much the freemen, engaged in the actual building operations, were paid we can only estimate roughly. Pliny says that the Claudian aqueduct cost over 350 million sesterces (or 25 million a year), which is a relatively modest amount for such a huge undertaking. Over 600,000 tons (tonnes) of squared tufa stone went into its construction. From this it is evident that labour costs were low, as they seemed to be still in A.D. 300.

The surveyors were probably better paid than most, as their job demanded exceptional skill and precision. Brick-making, because of the high cost of transport, was concentrated as near the City as possible. The great demand for bricks did not arise until the early Empire, when brick-faced, hard-mortar cores largely replaced travertine which, being a lime deposit, was found to crumble badly in a fire. There were many small brickworks employing up to about 50 slaves, each of whom could produce about 200 bricks a day. In the brick-making season from April to September one such collection of kilns might turn out a million bricks. This was the only industry open to aristocrats or patricians because it was regarded as a form of agriculture. In the whole of Roman history only one family is known to have attained political distinction after being made rich by industry in this way: bricks bearing the stamp of the orator Domitius Afer

118

remain as evidence of the wealth he created which helped the Antonine family to rise to imperial greatness. His great-granddaughter was the mother of the Emperor Marcus Aurelius.

CLOTHING

'Tunics, togas, blankets, smocks and shoes should be bought in Rome', said Cato in his manual on farming, so there was a well-established retail clothing trade from fairly early times alongside the larger domestic industry already described. Much of the woollen, linen and all the silk fabrics and furs used would have been imported. Fine clothing was sold in the Vicus Tuscus: 'Let my girl friend ask me for emeralds or a pound of rare perfume and not look at anything except fine silk from the Tuscan street', said Martial. Not that he could afford such luxuries, but he liked her to have good taste. Any material so bought would be made up either at home or by a little dressmaker or tailor in the City. Cheaper clothing might be had in several districts and we know from some inscriptions that there was quite a trade in old worn clothing which was turned into saddle cloths, quilts and wrappings—evident testimony to the relatively considerable cost of cloth.

Shoes were made in small workshops like those 'where many a cobbler blocks up the Argiletum' (54), as Martial said. The trade was specialised to the extent that some concentrated upon making heavy nailed boots, others, women's shoes and others, slippers. A reference has been found to a guild of 300 slipper-makers, which shows that there were many independent craftsmen. Lighter shoes were also made from plant fibres. Artificial materials and, of course, rubber were unknown.

MILLING AND BAKING

Difficult as it is to trace the origin and development of a commercial corn-grinding industry in Rome, there seems no doubt that it was becoming steadily more important in the later Republic. By the early days of the Empire the citizens of Rome seem already to have been largely dependent for their bread upon commercial bakeries (55), for it is recorded that, on one occasion, Caligula 'requisitioned waggons and so many animals from the bakeries that bread was frequently not to be had' in the Imperial City.

119

The commercial mills were enlarged versions of the hand mill or quern (p. 86). The only tolerably complete specimen of such a mill is that discovered under the ashes at Pompeii where four large mills were found in a row. They must have been turned by slaves because there was not enough room for an ass or a horse to turn them—these being the animals commonly used for all sorts of work in Rome. But it was the ass that was most used for turning the heavy mills (49). These mills were more clumsy than they need have been because the heavy hopper holding the grain above the grinding stones was also made of stone, although a lighter material such as wood or wicker would have been equally effective; but slaves and asses alike were expendable. Apuleius' *Golden Ass*, the strange story of the man who was changed into an ass, contains some gruesome descriptions of the merciless hard labour of slaves and asses in a flour mill. But perhaps the fact that Apuleius could invite Romans to imagine the sufferings of an ass and of the slaves in such a place is evidence that imaginative sympathy was possible even in Rome. We have no means of knowing whether the horrible conditions he describes were very general. What is certain is that an industry which had always been carried on first by women and then commercially by slaves and animals was regarded as of poor repute. Nothing but abject poverty drove a free citizen to the mills. The Roman playwright Plautus around 200 B.C. had been forced at one time through poverty, and as a last resort, to grind corn for a living.

At Rome some millers began to harness the Tiber, probably in the early years of the second century A.D., but water milling never rivalled the mills driven by animals or men. When Rome's long supremacy was nearing its end at the close of the fourth century A.D., an account of the 14 regions of the city was compiled from which a rough idea may be gathered of the total number of mills of all sorts, those attached to bakeries, those in large private houses and those in which the State authorities had corn ground. The total number has been variously estimated as between 230 and 317 mills. Now the water mills were almost all across the Tiber under the Janiculum Hill in district No. 14, where there were some 20 to 30 mills of all sorts. So it is clear that in an industry as vital as milling, the main motive force available to mankind, even in a City able to boast of a record of

49 Ass and slaves at work in a flour mill

human achievement greater than any hitherto realised in the history of the West, remained human and animal muscular energy.

This example from an industry on which the million or more Romans depended for their daily food, may serve as an illustration of the reasons for the lack of technical progress in Rome. It highlights the contrast between the virtually complete dependence of the Romans on muscular energy and our reliance upon machines to revolutionise the conditions of human existence. The following estimate made in the United States before atomic energy had begun to be harnessed effectively to industrial undertakings shows how rapidly things have changed there in a hundred years.

ENERGY PRODUCED IN THE UNITED STATES

Year	By men	By animals	By machines
1850	13%	52·4%	34·6%
1950	0·9%	0·6%	98·5%

In some industries automation has already led to the elimination of human labour to a greater degree than even these very striking figures suggest. In Rome the percentage of energy produced by machinery would have been as negligible as that of human and animal power combined in the U.S.A. today.

MARKET-GARDENING IN AND AROUND ROME

The country round about Rome served increasingly as time went on as the market garden of the City, for flowers and for green vegetables such as cabbages, lettuces, endives, asparagus, globe artichokes, parsley, mint and a great number of others no longer much used as food or flavouring such as the nasturtium. Among the many root-crops were radishes, turnips, parsnips, leeks, garlic, beet, skirrets and onions, as well as a number of bulbs and a root such as elecampane which is not now used for food, although the Romans thought well of it as a flavouring. Cucumbers and gourds were also grown.

Many varieties were distinguished among crops such as cabbages, lettuces and radishes, and from all of them and other plants a whole range of medicines and remedies was concocted. Pliny devoted many rolls of his *Natural History* to recording their virtues in illness. The lettuce was supposed to yield 42 remedies; parsley, 17; rye, 84; aniseed, 61, and so forth. No extended practical tests seem ever to have been made to discover what, if any, may be the merits of all this ancient lore about the healing properties of plants, some of which may not be so utterly wrong and fantastic as it seems.

The deep-rooted love of flowers, which is still a delightful aspect of life in Rome, created a large market for them. From the gardens and greenhouses of neighbouring Paestum, Tibur, Tusculum and Praeneste, flowers were brought to Rome in such profusion that Martial said the streets were so red with them that a sailor from Egypt, the famed home of flowers, would begin to get a mean opinion of the gardens of his native land. But there was nothing like the variety of flowers that we have today, and many of the blooms sold in Rome would probably seem little better than wild flowers to us. Nevertheless, they were probably more in demand then than in our own day, for every religious festival led to a demand for floral wreaths and offerings. Not on the many festival days alone, but on the three divisions of each month, the Kalends, Nones and Ides, every domestic shrine, with its *lares*, was crowned with flowers. The poor had to be content with laurel leaves or the cheapest wild flowers, but the richer would buy violets, lilies, roses and sweet-smelling herbs.

Every special family festival to celebrate birthdays and weddings led to a feast and no feast was complete without flowers. Then, as today, the displays would depend mainly on the wealth of the householders. The very rich went to extravagant lengths, having pretty slaves to strew the floor from lavish baskets of flowers and providing graceful crowns and chaplets of flowers for their guests. Dinner time was the 'hour of the rose'. Even those whose means were more modest, such as Horace, made it a point of honour to decorate the room and his guests with flowers, although his occasional extravagance on a special celebration, such as the birthday of Augustus, was no sign of that 'Oriental luxury', as he called it, for which he had a great aversion. When a girl-friend, Phyllis, was invited, she was promised ivy and parsley from his garden for the wreath for her hair. Horace was getting middle-aged. In his young days, he had known wilder moments. In a very well-known and much-translated ode, he asks one fair charmer what slender youth, crowned with many roses, is now pursuing her. Then, as in later times, lovers were as lavish with flowers as they could afford to be and love-lorn swains adorned the door and threshold of their lady-loves with garlands of flowers or leaves.

SHOPS AND MARKETS

In Rome's early days the relatively few inhabitants were largely self-sufficient, drinking water rather than wine and growing for themselves all they needed to eat. Some buying and selling soon began as the seven hills were covered with houses. Then the Romans used more and more to go down to the little narrow valley between the hills. There they met for business both private—to buy and sell—and public—to discuss matters of common interest and to hold councils of war, to decide disputes and to listen to the voice of authority. So this meeting place, where most people would be found at some time or other, soon became the centre of the city and some stalls or shops were set up there. Here also were the money-changers and money-lenders, for already people from neighbouring towns and villages were coming to Rome with their own coins to buy salt. Salt could be had only by evaporating sea-water, which was done easily on the flat coast about fifteen miles from Rome. To get to the salt pans, it was necessary to pass through Rome and lands con-trolled by the Romans, which greatly helped Roman trade.

The Romans spoke of 'the old shops' on the south side and 'the new shops' on the north side of the Forum which had been rebuilt in 210 B.C. after a disastrous fire. But soon these shops were not large enough. In 184 B.C. when there were already a quarter of a million free male inhabitants of Rome, a meeting place for business men, or basilica, was built by Cato, and another was added in 179 B.C. They were badly needed for now, more than ever, the *Forum Romanum* (p. 18) was the hub and centre of Roman public business. If you needed market news, political gossip and opinion, it was always to the Forum that you went for it. If mere idle curiosity prompted you, then the Forum was the place from which in Ancient Rome you got the sort of news and opinions now looked for in the gossip-columns of newspapers. The Romans never had newspapers as we know them today, but after 59 B.C. the *Acta Diurna* published important political and social news daily. It was hand-written.

50 A pharmacy
From a votive stele

TYPICAL SMALL SHOPS

51 A retail merchant's shop
From a bas-relief on a funeral monument

When, in the last two centuries of the Republic, the Forum was more and more used for public affairs, it became badly congested, the shops were crowded out and were forced to find room nearby. In Cicero's day the number of free male citizens had risen to nearly a million, but they did not all live in the City although most of them probably visited it at some time or another. Julius Caesar tackled the problem in an imaginative way, bought up the land on the north side of the Forum, pulled down all the houses and began to build an impressive brand-new square and market, the *Forum Julii* which his nephew Augustus completed and extended by his own *Forum Augusti*. It was from this time that the magnificence of Imperial Rome can be said to have begun. Not long afterwards, Nero was said to have founded a great market. More magnificent and larger than these imperial squares was the market (*52*) built by the Emperor Trajan (A.D. 114) adjoining the markets of Julius Caesar and Augustus. One side of it was built into the Quirinal hill which was partly dug away to make room for some of the 150 shops which the market housed. Large specialised and wholesale markets were mostly near the river, to be near the barges which brought in many of the vast supplies needed every day. The cattle market, *Forum boarium*, was south-west of the Forum on the low-lying land between the capital and the river Tiber. The main market for vegetables and fruit, the *Forum holitorium*, was next to it, also along the river, as were the oil merchants. The fish market in earlier times was unpleasantly close to the Forum. Its stinking fish was said in one of the plays of Plautus to drive all

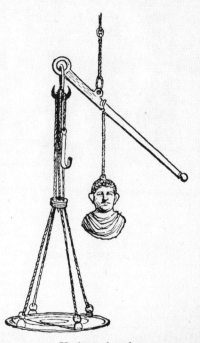

53 A steelyard

52 The *Forum Trajani*, the market built by the Emperor Trajan in A.D. 114

the loungers in the Basilica into the Forum. In addition there were very many large warehouses, some of them specialising in particular commodities such as paper, candles, oriental spices and so on.

Certain streets became famous for their special shops. The street of the Etruscans, *vicus Tuscus* in Imperial times, has been mentioned as one of the great shopping streets of Rome. All kinds of small shops were to be found in it, fishmongers, fruiterers and shops selling scents and perfumes(50) and the best silks. Elegant Romans, who always despised trade and shop-keepers, gave the street a bad name. As early as the days of Plautus the traders in this 'Etruscan' Street were said to be so keen to make money that they would sell themselves.

As Rome prospered and expanded to become the capital of the entire known world throughout the first four centuries of our era, the specialisation of its shopkeepers became more pronounced, just as has happened in London, New York, Paris, and other large cities. At the height of Rome's magnificence in

these later times book-sellers and leather sellers, who both made use of the same raw material were, no doubt for that reason, found together in the *Argiletum* running northwards from the Forum towards the working-class district of the Subura. That was a place to avoid. Crowded, noisy, dirty, smelly, it was also full of little shops where the poorer people of Rome went for their eggs, cabbages, bread and the few bare necessities of life, which was all they

54 A cobbler

could afford. There also were to be found many barbers, cobblers(54), ironmongers, and shops selling cheaper fabrics, all thronged by a jostling motley crowd among which were many slaves on errands for their masters and mistresses. For it seems as though most Romans, like the Parisians of modern times, either themselves or through their slaves, had to fetch and carry most of what they needed from the market. The difference is that women left the shopping to the men except for jewellery, clothes and luxury goods for themselves. There were not the same daily deliveries of milk and bread or regular supplies of groceries sent round to the door as there are in the Anglo-Saxon world.

While much of these busy shopping scenes would not look strange to anyone today, particularly to anyone who has seen Italian cities with their little shops, stalls and booths open to the street, some of the sights and smells would seem very odd. A pig in a baker's shop would astonish a Londoner or a Parisian but in Rome, particularly in the early Republic, where bakers had to grind their wheat before they could get flour for their bread, it was no uncommon sight to see a pig eating the baker-miller's bran in the streets, 'which stinks so much that nobody can pass by a baker's shop', said a character in a play by Plautus. Like the cows and sheep in Hyde Park, these picturesque links between the City and the country soon became things of the past.

PROFESSIONAL LIFE

None of the ways of earning a living referred to briefly above would have been regarded as suitable for a Roman lad of good family. Among the learned professions, the Romans gave little honour to any except the lawyers, because it was among them that they found their political leaders, or magistrates as they are called. Exceptionally, a great writer such as Virgil would be honoured in his lifetime purely as a literary man, but others, even Cicero, owed their contemporary fame to their oratory and not to their books. A literary man like Ovid or Martial does not seem to have been able to advance his social standing very much by his writings, however popular they may have become in his own lifetime. Most architects, doctors, surgeons and dentists would never fully overcome the stigma of having been slaves or freedmen.

127

'A good man skilled in speaking' was Cato's description of a lawyer in the middle of the second century B.C. The Roman habit of going to law was then already well developed and most Roman boys of good families were expected to learn how to defend a friend or client, or to prosecute a rival or an enemy. It was also the best, if not the only, way of entering the political arena, because trials were always held in public, in the Forum. Successful pleaders soon became known and so able to collect public votes if they stood for election to the annually vacant political offices. To be elected to one of these was the way to a seat in the Senate and perhaps to yet higher office either in Rome or in one of Rome's provinces.

So at the age of 17, after a young man laid aside his tunic with its purple stripe to assume the plain white manly toga, he would be led by a festive band of friends to be formally presented in public as a speaker in the law courts. His family would try to get a man of distinction in the State, if possible a consul or former consul, to act as his sponsor. Before this solemn ceremony, and indeed long afterwards, the lad would be expected to pick up as much knowledge of legal procedure and of the laws of Rome as he was able to do. Throughout the Republic there was only one way to get such training and that was by diligent attendance upon some older man who was already a successful pleader or lawyer. Cicero's father, for example, had friends in the *Pontifex Maximus* of his day, Publius Mucius Scaevola, and his cousin an Augur, from whom young Marcus was able to learn the rules and the skills of the legal profession and how to face the judges and the praetor in the Forum.

By the end of the Republic, legal business kept many distinguished Romans hard at work. Lawsuits were heard before a panel of anything up to 50 or 60 *judices* chosen from a list of about 4,000 of the upper classes, presided over by a praetor, one of the senior magistrates. The *judices* were a jury, but they had more influence than a British jury, which is merely asked to come to an impartial judgement on the facts in dispute, leaving the British judge to state and interpret points of law. The Roman *judices* were not so restricted. Their wider latitude had very important effects on Roman legal development because verdicts depended upon their judgement. Cold logic and a weight of legal learning, valuable as they no doubt were then as now, were not enough. The lawyer or advocate sought by spell-binding oratorical talent to capture the sympathies and interest of the jurymen. A theatrical element quite out of place in a British court of law was a common feature of Roman pleading.

To gain a mastery of legal learning, the young Roman had to become familiar with the laws of Rome, judicial forms and procedure, judgements and legal decisions of the praetor's courts year after year, as well as the text-books and learned treatises by experts on special points of law. He had also to be aware of the immemorial custom to which Romans were always ready to defer. The praetor's decisions were specially important because they did not merely expound, illustrate and apply existing law, as the judges do in English common law; they were able to introduce subtle modifications of the law itself. Under the weight of all this learning, the legal profession became more formalised and specialised as time went on, and it split into two main specialities. A body of legal consultants grew up having great knowledge of the law but no inclination or ability to face the rough-and-tumble of the courts. Clients and their advocates would go to them for briefing upon knotty points of law and they would expect fees for their advice. The advocates who undertook to present and argue the case in court, however, could not demand and were not supposed to expect fees. Their reward came indirectly in the shape of 'presents' or perhaps legacies. The *judices* and the praetor were also unpaid, but there was strong competition to join their ranks because of the influence and social standing so to be gained. The very influential position of the *judices* explains why there was such a row when Gaius Gracchus replaced senators by business men as *judices* in the court before which senatorial provincial governors could be brought on charges of extortion.

By the end of the Empire, lawyers, like many of the other inhabitants of Rome, seem to have suffered from a weakening of their moral standards. Bribery of jurors was not indeed unknown earlier: Cicero already had occasion to denounce it as a sign of the fundamental political rottenness of his days.

If we may believe Ammianus Marcellinus who wrote at the end of the fourth century A.D., he had witnessed a bad slump. 'We see the most violent and rapacious classes of men', he lamented, 'besieging the houses of the rich, cunningly creating lawsuits.' Indeed, he could find nothing good to say about the majority of the lawyers of his day. Many of them were so ignorant that 'if in the company of learned men the name of any ancient author is mentioned, they fancy it to be the name of some foreign fish or eatable'. What was worse, 'doors are now daily more and more opened to plunder by the depravity of judges and advocates who are all alike and who sell the interests of the poor to the military commanders'. Roman law had, however, taken shape by this time and it was able to survive evils as great as these. Despite the crippling influence of Imperial despotism and the recurrent threats of imminent collapse, Roman law continued to exhibit a vigour and a vitality that have ensured its survival over large parts of Europe as a basis of that Rule of Law which is among the more enduring titles of the Roman Republic to lasting cultural renown.

Doctors

'The Romans', said Pliny, in the first century A.D., 'got along without doctors for 600 years.' If it had not been for the Greeks they might well never have had any. The old school of Romans in the days of Cato and Cicero's grandfather mistrusted and despised the Greeks. Never having had any doctors at all, they were certainly not likely to trust newcomers from Greece. 'Out with the Greeks' was a slogan which long raised sympathetic echoes in some circles in Republican Rome. By sheer merit, the Greeks slowly won through to recognition, at least from intelligent Romans. Scipio Africanus, Scipio Aemilianus, and Gaius Gracchus were among the outstanding Romans of the second century B.C. who took the lead in bringing Greek culture to Rome. They prepared the way for Cicero, who in the following century often declared his profound admiration for the Greeks and his great debt to them: 'A race of men', he said, 'in whom civilisation not only exists but from whom it is believed to have spread to others.' So also, 'first came a man from Greece', proclaimed Lucretius, the most deeply reflective and philosophical of Latin poets. Alone among the peoples of the

130

Mediterranean, the Romans proved willing and able to value and absorb what the Greeks had to teach.

In so far as reliance upon herbs and salts was able to supplement the ministrations of priests and holy persons, it was through the head of each household that they were applied. The father of the house, the *paterfamilias*, was the high priest who collected the remedies and kept them in the store cupboard under the benign influence of the household gods, the *penates*. Rare, strange and revolting were some of the powders and potions so treasured: gladiator's blood, animal dung and urine, human fat, infant's brains, seal's rennet, and countless others. The more exotic and repulsive they were, the more trust they inspired; *omne ignotum pro magnifico*, as Tacitus summed up this universal human failing. There was therefore at least some resource for the afflicted in addition to the mystic laying-on of hands, the ritual bindings and loosenings, the muttering of names and incantations, the respect for mystic numbers, the use of holy wells, springs, baths, the anointings with holy water, temple sleep, sacrifices, votive offerings and the interpretation of dreams, all of which entered largely into human reactions to disease. Among many disgusting and worse than useless concoctions and some gibberish by way of incantations, some elements of sanity were to be found. Cato relied considerably upon the cabbage, which as a source of vitamin C undoubtedly had its virtues in the otherwise restricted diet of the Romans, especially in winter months.

When the Greek physician, either as a slave in a rich household or as a free- or freedman practising for a living, replaced the father of the household, the beginnings of some specialised skill and knowledge at last became available to the Romans. Julius Caesar in 46 B.C. gave Roman citizenship to all practising doctors. It was unfortunately just as easy for any charlatan or quack to step into the position of trusted physician and to bluff his way through by a combination of effrontery and pseudo-learning. Large fortunes were to be made in this way. 'A physician', said the Elder Pliny, 'is the only man who can kill anyone with sovereign impunity ... to this however we pay no attention, so alluring is the hope of a cure.' No record remains of the vast numbers of unfortunate men, women and children who came to an untimely end at the hands of such scoundrels.

131

Never in the history of Rome were courses of instruction and the award of diplomas after careful examination made a condition for the lawful practice of medicine as it is among us today. Doctors got their training by watching those already in practice. 'I was feeling ill when you attended me, Symmachus, with a hundred apprentices. A hundred hands frozen by the north wind pawed me. I had no fever then, but now I have,' complained Martial.

Against the firmly entrenched nonsense of the Romans the best of the Greeks went armed by the inspiration of Hippocrates, who in the fifth century B.C. accepted the popular belief that 'all diseases are divine in origin and that no malady is more divine or human than another', but added the all-important consideration that 'each has its own nature and does not arise without natural causes'. Slowly merit and genius made some temporary gains at the expense of ignorance, superstition and greed. The first of the renowned Greeks to win fame and fortune in Rome was Asclepiades, whose active career in Rome, where he arrived in 91 B.C., covered the lifetime of Cicero. Failing to succeed as a teacher of rhetoric, according to Pliny the Elder, he suddenly switched to medicine about which he knew little or nothing. Discarding the worst of the remedies of the old traditional folk-medicine of Rome, he laid greater emphasis upon more natural methods, paying special attention to diet, exercise, fresh air, light, massage, baths and regular and sensible ways of living. He also won no mean fame as a surgeon. Evidently he had an excellent 'bedside manner' and owed much of whatever success he achieved to neglecting the old cures rather than to thinking of new ones. Considering that he was the first to confront and oppose the whole entrenched might of contemporary dogmatism and superstition, his achievements must have indeed been great.

After the great work of Galen in the time of Marcus Aurelius, medical progress was over. Superstition and old-wives' remedies were preferred to scientific endeavour. Oriental demonism and magic gained the day. Whatever benefits medicine may have offered in Ancient Rome, they were very unevenly shared, for the poor had little or no access to the best doctors and, apart from military establishments, there were no hospitals or clinics available to treat them until a few were provided under Christian

55 A baker's shop

From a Pompeian wall-painting of the first century, A.D.

inspiration at the end of the Empire. One or two doctors seem to have accepted patients at their homes, but most Romans died at home, many with the minimum of care or attention. In the first century A.D. Seneca said that the dying were left alone. 'No one sits with a dying friend. None can bring himself to witness the death of his father, however much he wishes for it.' Yet the need for defence against illness grew greater as the simple old Roman life on the land gave way to sophisticated City ways and as new diseases such as malaria rose from the marshes of the once-fertile plains of Latium and the Campagna. Typhus, dysentery, tuberculosis, smallpox, anthrax, rabies, tetanus, plague, were all apt to rage and to take a heavy toll from the defenceless Romans. Not merely had they no cure for such maladies, but such was their lack of any truly scientific curiosity that they made no effort by experiment or research to discover cures. That unusually energetic Roman enquirer, Pliny the Elder, complained that 'in the blessed peace which we enjoy under an Emperor who takes such pleasure in the progress of the world and of the arts, no addition whatever is being made to knowledge by original research, neither even are the discoveries of our predecessors being thoroughly studied'. As he said, the rewards would have been great; he concluded that men had become lazy and degenerate.

Surgeons

Surgery, through long practice by trial and error and some practice in dissection, had reached a considerable proficiency. Some 200 surgical instruments of various kinds have been discovered at Pompeii (57). Fractures and dislocations could be treated skilfully. Artificial legs were not unknown. The use of the knife to remove abcesses and to clear up pleurisy was competent. The absence of anaesthetics and of antisepsis added tremendously to the shock and the risks of such treatment at the hands of even expert surgeons. The number of lives sacrificed by more clumsy operators, and by men trying to acquire some skill, may plausibly be believed to have been great. There was as yet no hint of the marvels of modern surgery and even operations now regarded as relatively simple, such as appendicitis, were far beyond Roman skills. Greater attention was, however, paid to manipulative surgery than has been general in modern times.

56 The interior of the Temple of Jupiter Capitolinus, rebuilt by Sulla in 82 B.C.
From a reconstruction by Giuseppe Gatteschi

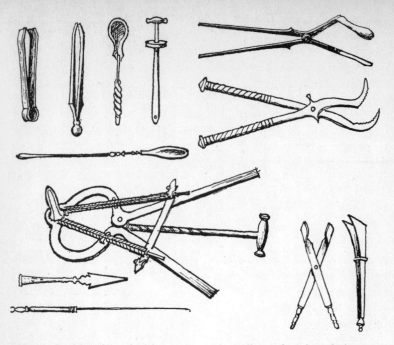

57 A selection of surgical instruments, including a four-jawed clamp

Romans able to afford it could receive thoroughly expert massage. Anything from four to six masseurs got to work on the body at once, stepping up their treatment from a slow and gentle beginning to a quicker and more powerful conclusion. Many also sought to achieve and preserve good muscular tone and physical efficiency through curative gymnastics, which the Greeks had early brought to perfection. Such treatments, allied with the frequent use of cold and very hot baths, with spa waters and exercise at the ball game or in the hunting field, kept many Romans in much better physical condition than is the average city business man today.

Very little seems to have been recorded about dentistry among the Romans. The Etruscans had, however, some very skilled dentists. In the Twelve Tables of Roman Law, it was allowed that anyone 'whose teeth shall have been fastened together (*juncti*) with gold' shall be an exception from the law that prevented gold being buried with a corpse. Now if, as it seems, this is a reference to skilled dentistry, it is very early (about 450 B.C.). Cicero mentions one of the gods who was supposed to have taught the Greeks how to draw teeth. Pliny has many remedies for toothache, one of which at least, *plantago*, is still recommended by homeopaths today. Toothpaste was regularly used by those who could afford it. *Nitrum*, probably either potassium or sodium carbonate, was burnt and rubbed on the teeth to restore their colour. Blackened and stained teeth were common and were often mentioned with disgust by Martial, who also has several references to false teeth and to dentists. 'Cascellius draws or stops the decayed tooth,' he said.

Writers

There is no evidence to show how much direct benefit authors may have gained from the circulation of their works or whether they got, as most authors do today, a small percentage or 'royalty' on every copy sold. From the recommendations to buy his poems from the booksellers Atrectus or Tryphon, it would seem that Martial gained something from their sale, although he said his books 'were thumbed by the hardy centurion among Getic frosts, beside martial standards, and Britain is said to hum my verses. What profit's that? My purse knows nothing of it.' There is no doubt that the booksellers profited. Then, as now, authors did not write to make money only but were often satisfied to have their productions circulated, in the hope of getting their views discussed and perhaps of succeeding thereby in influencing other minds to accept opinions and beliefs which they themselves regarded as true and important. Many wrote, and even gave public recitations, in the hope of gaining fame, rather in the way that some authors now appear on television programmes. Cicero, who had his eye also on far distant posterity, said that he was much more concerned about the opinion likely to be taken of him hundreds of years after his death than he was over the chatter about him by his contemporaries.

More tangible rewards might be showered upon men who achieved fame by their writings and by their oratory. Their excellence was sometimes acknowledged in a way that many later writers would very much like to see revived: they were left legacies by grateful admirers. Cicero benefited very considerably by such posthumous generosity and he made it a point of honour to boast about his good fortune. Virgil and Horace in the following generation did not have to wait until their rich friends died, but they found a living patron in Maecenas, the trusted friend of the Emperor Augustus, and they were able to lead a life of leisure as a result of his and the Emperor's kindness.

Memory of such favours encouraged later writers to hope for similar benefits, and to dip their pens into sharp acid when they were not forthcoming, were deferred, or were small. 'Let there be many a Maecenas and we shall not lack for many Virgils,' said Martial, although he knew it was not true. Yet he makes no secret of his hope for patronage. 'What immortal pages could I not have written', he said, 'if the kind deities had given Rome a second Maecenas.' Some rich men included writers in the circle of their clients in later times, but never again were patrons as generous and discerning as Maecenas and Augustus. Later Emperors sometimes found jobs for men with literary ability, but this was not the same thing as the leisured ease of Virgil or Horace.

If society has any duty towards gifted writers and orators, it is unlikely to be acknowledged adequately in a practical way during their lifetime. Plautus, Terence, Catullus, Cicero, Lucretius, Virgil, Horace, Livy, Ovid, Tacitus and other Roman writers, whose fame and circle of readers have grown ever vaster through the centuries, obviously could not have shared in the enormous capital value which their writings can be said to have created. But this is true of all geniuses and it is silly to try to put a cash value on their creations.

FREE FOOD

Thousands, perhaps hundreds of thousands, of Romans were so dangerously near the poverty-line that merely to get enough bread each day was their major ambition in life. Despite the great power and wealth of Rome during the Empire, this canker of chronic poverty remained to plague its rulers and to diminish the lustre of their Imperial glory. To understand it involves a bit of history, because it was an old problem that had grown steadily more acute ever since subsistence-farming ceased to be practical economics in the immediate vicinity of Rome during the second century B.C. Few of Rome's leaders had any conscience about the growing landless proletariat whose small plots had been swallowed, either by large-scale cattle breeders who alone could make the land pay, or by suburban builders who, from an agricultural point of view, destroyed the land. In the second half of the second century B.C. the problem was tackled in a determined manner by two aristocrats, the brothers Tiberius and Gaius Gracchus. Their fate, like that of many who tried to help the poor at the expense of the rich, was to be murdered by their aristocratic opponents, but not before the youngest, Gaius Gracchus, had laid the foundation for the only remedy the Romans ever found for the chronic poverty of thousands of Roman citizens. He arranged in 123 B.C. that once a month the government of the Republic should sell 5 *modii*, or about 72 lb. (37 kilos), of wheat to every citizen at the price of 6⅓ *asses*—a price roughly equal to its cost of production in Sicily and Africa. The State had to pay for its transport and of course any excess, if, owing to poor crops, the price rose above this guaranteed price. The State could easily afford such a scheme, which was financed not at the expense of the richer Romans but by the provinces, who were taxed, whereas throughout the greater part of the second and first centuries B.C. the Romans no longer paid taxes. It had always been a recognised duty of the Roman Republic to ensure an adequate supply of grain for its citizens. The Gracchi, whose whole outlook infuriated the tradition-bound, tight-fisted Romans, who hated any such interference in economic life, had other more drastic plans to 'share the wealth' by reviving old limits upon large estates. The enemies they made by their schemes succeeded in murdering them, but the plan for selling a limited amount of wheat to Roman citizens remained. Conservative efforts to abolish it were not very resolute except under the dictator Sulla in 82 B.C. Neither did Sulla's reform last very long. Trouble began when, in order to get

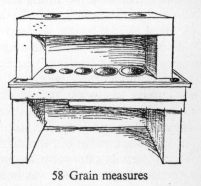

58 Grain measures

political support for Julius Caesar, his demagogue supporter Clodius promoted a law to give the wheat away free. Gracchus in his most expansive mood had never proposed that. Soon 320,000 Romans then, for the first time, had their basic food supply free of charge and at other people's expense. Caesar was responsible for the corn dole, just as he was for lavish free entertainment for the mob. 'Bread and Circus shows' were Caesar's demagogic methods of keeping Romans happy, perhaps temporarily, until he could work out long-term plans. The result was that poor farmers near Rome gave up the struggle to grow their own miserable food supply and flocked to Rome. As the free corn dole was only given to citizens, a number of slave owners freed their slaves, so that they no longer would need to feed them. An idle half-fed city proletariat was rapidly increased in this way. If it is untrue that all men would be parasites if they could, the history of Rome shows that it was frighteningly true of most of them.

After the fierce Civil War between Julius Caesar and Pompey and his Republican supporters, Caesar had to grapple with the tremendous problem he had created. For 12 years most of the citizens of Rome had been getting free wheat. They were, in Cicero's words, 'the wretched starving mob, the bloodsuckers of the Treasury'. Caesar reduced the list to 150,000 names. He was able to do so without provoking a revolt, partly because he was supreme as Dictator and partly because he could strike off the thousands who had died or been killed in the Civil wars, as well as the 80,000 citizens he had sent to live in Roman colonies or provinces. For the future he tried to keep the cost within bounds by adding new names to the free list only when vacancies occurred by the death of former recipients. Such newcomers were chosen by lot from the long lists of applicants. The result was two distinct classes of Roman citizens, those with a right to free corn and those without it, but his plan for economy did not survive his assassination. Corn again became a political weapon and, despite his dislike for it, Caesar's successor, Augustus the first Emperor, not only maintained the dole but increased the number of beneficiaries to the old figure of 320,000 (5 B.C.). Shortly afterwards he brought it back to 200,000, but the tendency all the time was to allow it to increase. Augustus admitted all citizens' sons over ten years of age. By the end of the first century A.D. Trajan allowed every son of any age to benefit, hoping to stimulate the growth of population. It was, however, still a privilege confined to Roman citizens resident in Rome, a fact which distinguished the recipients from 'sordid plebeians'. So much so that it was sometimes mentioned with pride on tombstones that the defunct had enjoyed the right to the corn dole. Many of those living in Rome still had to buy their corn on the open market. But it seems that, as might be expected, there was a black market on which it was possible to buy a citizen's grain ticket, so no doubt there was considerable difficulty in controlling the system of free doles of corn. Throughout the Empire, despite the wealth and power of Rome, the corn-dole problem was never solved: as an early experiment in State socialism it certainly had far from brilliant results.

Before the time of trouble and decay in the Empire from the third century A.D. onwards, the Roman way of life had undergone a great change, although the changes were not as amazing and spectacular as those in the British or French way of life between the twelfth and nineteenth centuries. The Romans' early period of somewhat primitive simplicity and austerity might have lasted very much longer but for their success in making themselves masters of the known world. But the riches they acquired by foreign conquest were unevenly shared at home and they could not guarantee permanent prosperity. The difference between the standard of living of poor and rich grew greater in all respects as time went on. As Rome filled up and lodgings became more expensive, the poor had to go to cheaper and more miserable attics and hovels, existing rather than living in one-room apartments in mean buildings, without water, hearth or fire. What did they do with their 72 lb. of free wheat each month? They would not find it easy to store and few could grind it or cook it. They must have been compelled to entrust it to some baker-miller to turn into food. Although many had this free grain, they would not get a good hot meal unless they were invited out by some richer friends or patrons, or unless they had money to spend at a little cook-shop where they might buy a snack along with a cup of warm wine.

139

These little eating and drinking houses(59) had many names. Corresponding to our pubs, taverns, inns, cafes and cabarets the Romans had their *cauponae*, *popinae* and *tabernae vinariae*. They were to be found all over Rome and were often cheap resorts, catering mainly for the poor and for slaves: 'dirty', 'greasy', 'smoky' and 'grimy' is how Cicero, Virgil and Horace refer to them. A wall painting at Pompeii depicts the customers sitting round on stools, but we read also about the violent brawls which broke out in them. Because of such scenes and because of the morbid fear that any gathering of Romans would lead to a conspiracy against the government, reforming Emperors such as Tiberius struck at them by forbidding them to sell even pastry. Claudius is reported to have tried to close them entirely, a story not very consistent with the tale told by Suetonius that the garrulous Emperor had intervened during a debate in the Senate about butchers and wine merchants saying, 'I ask you, who can live without a snack?', rambling on to talk about the great number of such wine-shops in the old days and how he used to go to them for drinks. His step-son and successor, Nero, prohibited the cookshops from selling any hot food except vegetables and herbs, 'whereas before', says Suetonius, 'every

59 An inn scene

kind of relish was to be had'. A rule of this kind was unpopular and difficult to enforce, as can be gathered from the fact that it was renewed by the Emperor Vespasian.

ROMAN ROADS

Their straight paved roads remain among the enduring contributions of the Romans to Western civilisation. In the 300 years after the *via Appia* of 312 B.C. first gave Rome a good highway to the south, all parts of Italy were connected to Rome by excellent metalled roads. This was new in human history. Road-making continued throughout the Empire so that in the next 400 years the Roman provinces were covered by a network of military roads usually soundly based on flagstones, gravel and concrete. Built so that Rome's legions could move swiftly through any province, they soon gave excellent service in trade, commerce and social travel. Of all Rome's material achievements, none did so much to aid the spread of civilisation and culture, or the Romanisation of the West than these roads.

CLASS DISTINCTIONS

Class divisions in Roman society, as this and the previous chapter show, were very real. People were inferior or superior and they knew it. Throughout antiquity there was first the sharp division between slave and free. The slaves were always the largest class of inferiors. Above them, but low in the free social scale, were the freed men and the poor citizens who were workmen or humble clients of the rich. The higher class divisions changed in the course of Rome's history. In early times service to the Republic as magistrate or successful commander in battle greatly enhanced a man's social standing. Distinction of this sort remained and indeed descended to dignify sometimes worthless descendants. Later it was overlaid to some extent by successes in other fields, such as oratory (e.g. Cicero), acting (Roscius), literature (Virgil) and, for the mob, in the circus or arena. Wealth alone could earn distinction after the second century B.C. It could buy an army of slaves and poor clients. Thereafter the Emperor overshadowed everybody, able to give or to take away social distinction as he pleased. The story of Rome's early class struggles between plebeians and patricians, poor and rich, slaves and free, belongs to political history.

141

Chapter VI

LEISURE HOURS

THE Romans' working week was not one of seven days, but of eight. The eighth day was counted, by inclusive reckoning, as the ninth and was called *nundinae*, the whole week of eight days being *internundinum*. From very early times, after seven days' work in the fields the farmers broke off on the eighth day and went to their small market towns. Later on, every *nundinae* was a holiday for the citizens of Rome, except for the stallholders in the markets who, as in French towns on Sundays today, had a busy time.

The days of the year were also divided into those favourable to work and business, *dies fasti*, and those unfavourable, *dies nefasti*. On the latter, though the ordinary business of buying and selling was probably little affected, public affairs were suspended and the lawcourts shut. Worse still were the 'black days', *dies atri*, the anniversaries of Roman defeats and disasters, for, unlike other nations, the Romans remembered and mourned their defeats and disasters. On them, as on the great public festivals, it was considered unlucky to undertake any business of importance. According to the great German scholar Mommsen, the Roman year contained 239 days specified as suitable for legal and political business, 48 *dies nefasti* and 51 *dies atri*. But a calendar discovered near Antium shows that in the Republican period only 192 days were suitable for public business, while 109 days were regarded as *nefasti*. Evidently some enlargement of permissible days must have become essential in the busier times of the Empire. But, even so, one day out of three might call for some observance even if it was not a public holiday.

The opportunities for leisure were not confined merely to such special days, because the normal working day lasted only six hours: those who had work stopped at midday, the seventh hour in the Roman day. Martial describes a Roman day beginning at sunrise with the first hour:

The first and second hour wearies clients at the levée, the third hour starts off the hoarse advocates, until the end of the fifth hour Rome carries on its manifold tasks, the sixth gives rest to the weary, the seventh will be the end. The eighth to the ninth is enough for the oiled wrestlers, the ninth bids us to throw ourselves on couches piled high with cushions.

Remembering that many jobs which free workers might have done were done by slaves and that much that we think essential was left undone, it is not surprising that in the heyday of Rome's greatness large numbers of people in Rome were under-employed or had no regular employment. Thousands seem to have survived on the charity of the rich, supplemented by the free wheat and water supplied by the State. To this number must be added the many people who had some income from rents, property or pensions and who came to Rome in the belief that they would get a much fuller and more exciting life in the capital city than anywhere else in the world.

THE LURE OF ROME

Life in Rome afforded an infinity of distractions compared with the dull daily routine of a country town or village. It was all very well for the poet Martial, in a dispirited hour, to ask who would weary himself in Rome paying court to the wealthy in their vast cold marble halls, when he could be rich with the spoils of woods and fields, catch all the fish he wanted, have red pots full of honey and cook his own new-laid eggs on charcoal which he did not have to buy from a dealer. Martial came to Rome in his early twenties, about A.D. 63 or 64, and spent most of his life there. Not till he was in his his sixties, in A.D. 100, did he go back to his native Spain where he died a year or two later. In less jaded mood, he knew how to enjoy himself in the City. Instead of flattering the rich or shouting himself hoarse in lawsuits in the Forum he would take a trip with a friend in a light carriage, or stroll through gardens and shady colonnades or round the bookshops and antique shops and the playing fields in the *Campus Martius*. He would seek refreshment from the fresh, cold water of the aqueducts, and society, amusement, as well as refreshment, in any of the four great *thermae* or Baths, of Agrippa, Nero, Gryllus and Titus. Later emperors were to add yet other *thermae*, to provide more gardens, more temples, arcades, market places, libraries and yet further to add to the amenities and to the attractions of Rome. For the average poor Roman the *thermae* provided opportunity for relaxation, for they were much more than 'baths'.

THE BATHS

Beginning in the second century B.C., when they were small, strictly practical 'wash-houses', and reserved for men only, public baths grew tremendously in size, in magnificence and in their amenities during the Empire. Merely to hint at their splendour fails to do justice to the impression they must have made upon all who saw them. The great majority of Romans, escaping from their small hovels or mean apartments to spend an hour or two or the whole day at one of the *thermae*, could not fail to be struck by the grandeur and beauty of these vast, richly decorated marble and gold palaces provided for their enjoyment. For the Baths were no longer simply buildings where anyone could, by paying one *quadrans* (the smallest Roman coin), have a bath; rather they were enormous recreation-centres, fully equipped with gymnasia, gardens, libraries and reading rooms in addition to the baths themselves.

The energy and resources devoted to their construction and adornment have no parallel in the public buildings of modern times in whose rigorously controlled and mean construction avoidable expense is carefully spared. Magnificence, beauty and

60 The *frigidarium* of the Baths of Caracalla

comfort were then the standards, not money-budgets and cost-accounting as today. We have to go back nearly three hundred years, to the erection of St. Paul's Cathedral, to find any modern public building in London comparable architecturally with the Roman Baths. It would have seemed small beside them. It occupies about 64,000 square feet (5945 sq. metres) and the height of the nave is about 100 feet (30·5 m). The main block alone of the Baths of Caracalla (A.D. 211–217), which was as high, covered 270,000 square feet (25,084 sq. metres), more than the Houses of Parliament. The Baths of Diocletian (A.D. 284–305) were considerably larger. They accommodated over 3,000 bathers at a time, about double the number catered for by Caracalla. They took ten years to build against the five devoted to the Baths of Caracalla. It was 35 years before St. Paul's was completed. Rome was by no means short of public Baths when these two sumptuous constructions were erected. Agrippa provided the first in A.D. 20. Thereafter we have remains of those of Nero (A.D. 54–68), Titus (A.D. 79–81), Trajan (A.D. 98–117), Trajanus Decius (A.D. 249–51), and Constantine (A.D. 306–337), in addition to those of Caracalla and Diocletian.

During the Empire the Baths were open to men, women and children alike, and even the very modest charge of one *quadrans* was sometimes remitted by the generosity of the Emperor or of a rich man, who might make himself responsible for the entire cost of the baths for anything from a day to a year. One set of rooms was provided for men and another for women, although there was also some mixed bathing in the days of Nero, greatly to the scandal of the sterner Romans. A succession of orders against such licence by the Emperors Hadrian, Marcus Aurelius and Alexander Severus is the best evidence that it was difficult or impossible to restrain. Romans went to the Baths to meet others, to stroll about and talk, some to play ball and other games, some to take yet more violent exercise such as wrestling(*61*) or to watch others at it, and of course to get cool in summer and warm in winter. There were cold baths in the *frigidarium*(*60*), a warm room or the *tepidarium* and a heated chamber, the *calidarium*, where there were warm baths and hot air to induce perspiration as in our modern Turkish bath. An even hotter room, the *laconicum*, was used mainly by invalids. The heat was provided by a fierce fire under the floors stoked

145

61 Bathers wrestling in a *palaestra*

by slaves with great quantities of wood. Bathers could enjoy any one or all of these in turn and in any order.

Part of the treatment was to remove bodily impurities thrown off by perspiration by being scraped down with a metal, bone or wooden *strigilis*(62), for the Romans lacked soap; 'scrape yourself with the curved blade', advised Martial, 'the fuller will not so often wear out your towels'.

The bathers either brought slaves with them to carry their towels, to scrape, and to rub them down, or they hired such services at the Baths where there were also masseurs, anointers, depilators and perfumers. The poor, who could afford none of these attentions, rubbed and scraped themselves by hand or against a wall. It has already been remarked (p. 144) how the Baths also became social centres. They were notorious for the noise coming from them, for Romans liked to sing in their baths, to whistle, to talk and shout at their friends and acquaintances. After reclaiming their tunics and togas from the cloakroom attendant, if they had not been stolen or replaced by shoddy worn-out clothes by some smart thief, as they sometimes were, they could lounge, talk and stroll, read or eat before they all went their ways: the rich in a closed litter and the poor on foot in the sun, rain or snow.

At first the Baths closed at sunset, but, from the multitude of lamps discovered in the Baths at Pompeii, it seems that bathing was extended into the night in the first century, although it is possible that the lamps were required merely to light otherwise dark corridors and enclosed rooms even in daytime. The Baths were set in gardens.

Like most of the cultural interests in the life of the Romans, their love of gardens had been inspired by Greek examples. The Greeks in turn seem to have got the idea after Alexander the Great's soldiers had seen the royal and princely gardens of Persia and the East. It was the Greeks who put gardens near or around their shrines, temples, porticoes, promenades and theatres, and the Romans copied them. It was something very new when outside

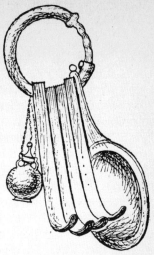

62 Masseur's oil-container, strigils and oil-pan

the first permanent theatre in Rome, built by Pompey around 60 B.C., a grove or strip of trees was added. Greek cities also had their public gardens. All these pleasant Greek practices were copied by the Romans so that during the Empire a number of public parks were created before the large *thermae* had been thought of. Julius Caesar bequeathed his gardens across the Tiber to the Roman people. When his successor Augustus died, a park was provided around his great Mausoleum. Augustus had already put a park around the great artificial lake he had created (the *Naumachia*) to stage the murderous naval battles, devised to vary the scenes of slaughter in which his subjects revelled. The older, purely Roman interest in a sacred grove of a few trees was enlarged and perpetuated in this way. The dark, black shade and coolness under thickly covered trees and bushes was especially valued for its sharp contrast with the glare and heat of a sunny Italian day.

HIGH SOCIETY

Martial's idea of the good life was that of an intelligent educated member of the middle classes. He shared as much as he could afford to do in the tastes of the wealthy aristocratic families who lived a life of their own, with its social round of visits and receptions, crowded busy days and equally busy evenings and nights with their succession of elegant, luxurious dinner parties. They were able to diversify city life by frequent trips to the country and seaside, staying with friends or in their own many country villas on the way. Their days were made effortless, thanks to the labours of their armies of slaves. Where so much was done to gratify their every whim and where their lives could, if they wished, be entirely given over to leisure, it might be expected that cultural life would flourish as never before. Yet there is little evidence that there was any such progress. The great Roman aristocrats of the Roman Empire produced no great literature, drama or music. They painted no pictures, they neither understood scientific research nor deep philosophical reflection, neither did they set other people to work in such ways. Their good taste drove up the price of antique furniture, silver and pictures to heights which astonished their contemporaries in the same way that fortunes are given today for the choicest of such rarities. Their morals and behaviour, the third great factor in cultural life, were sometimes inspired by the older severe traditions of the Republican times, but for the most part were 'no better than they ought to have been', as the saying goes, and often very much worse. The newly found freedom of Roman women (p. 61) helped to civilise Roman social life through the sumptuous dinner parties in which the wealthier Romans sought to dispel boredom. After the Baths closed at dusk what else could they do? The poor went home to eat and sleep, unless the man of the house had a meeting of his trade guild or burial club upon which many Romans had to rely to ensure a decent departure from this world. There were no evening concerts, dances, theatres, clubs, cafés, political, professional or other reunions at which people can now be brought together.

Well-to-do Romans therefore gave much of their time to dining in style, drinking and talking. In the more exclusive circles of the Roman aristocracy such grand dinner parties could be delightful occasions(63). The company would consist of three, six or nine at most, because not more than nine could recline comfortably at one table, while more than three tables would be liable to upset the unity of a dinner party, turning

63 A dinner party

it into a public banquet. The food would be well chosen, excellently prepared and cooked and very tastefully served by a team of thoroughly well-trained and attractive-looking slaves.

Over far too long periods, the principal and most acute difficulty during the elegant dinner parties of the aristocracy might well be to find safe topics of conversation. The aristocracy were near the Imperial Court and the Emperor, who was often to be feared and was sometimes a dangerous maniac. Such was the peril and uncertainty of the time that careless talk at a dinner party was a fearful risk. The least loose word, perhaps even the recital of a dream, might be carried to high places by an ill-disposed, covetous person anxious to curry favour at Court, even though he doomed an innocent fellow guest to a sudden and atrocious death. Except in the greater part of the golden, or gilded, second century A.D. this appalling danger was sufficiently real to poison much of the pleasure which lavish social living could have provided. A vigorous cultural life, as we have just seen, failed to develop, such is the high cost to human happiness and progress of arbitrary government and the tyranny and cruelty by which it is always apt to be accompanied.

To remain living quietly at home might also be dangerous for a prominent Roman because he would then immediately be suspected of disaffection by the Emperor's clique. The wealthier a man was, the greater risk he ran because if he could be condemned the Emperor might confiscate his property. An informer would expect some share of it also. The more prudent and serious well-to-do country families therefore kept away from Rome for their own safety and peace of mind, and for the moral welfare of their children. 'Oh, how many learned men are hidden and withdrawn from the world by their modesty and their preference for a quiet life,' said Pliny after a visit to one of his able neighbours in the country.

So the talk around the elegant dinner tables would turn upon the love affairs, divorces, and domestic scandals of other members of society, diversified by stories and jokes.

The grave, sober and serious attitude of much of Roman life, particularly among Romans of the old school is so characteristic that we are apt to forget their fun and humour and the frequent flashes of sarcasm and wit with which they enlivened their days and their dinner parties. Much of it was very direct, personal and blunt. Rather in the way of simple, uncultured people today they seemed to have considered any kind of personal oddity as extremely funny. A great number of their witty, smart sayings would consequently now be thought in rather poor taste. This characteristic comes out in many family names perpetuating down the ages some such special characteristic of a remote ancestor. Ahenobarbus, 'red-beard', was applied to the Domitian clan; Balbus, a stammerer, Claudius, the lame, Plautus, flat-feet, Paulus, little, Crassus fat. The names of animals were applied to others: Asinius, ass, Porcius, pig, Aper, boar, Vitellius, calf; while some had the names of plants: Cicero, chick-pea, Caepio, onion, Tubero, a truffle. These soon ceased to seem funny as people got used to them. A dinner table would repeat with relish some of the witty remarks of an urbane and cultivated man such as Cicero, who also could not resist making a joke of another's appearance. When he saw his son-in-law Dolabella, who was very short, walking about trailing a large sword, he asked 'who has fastened my son-in-law to that sword?' He did not even spare his brother Quintus who was also short, for, when he was shown the very large portrait bust made while his brother was governing as praetor in Asia Minor, he said: 'Here we have a part which is twice as great as the whole.'

The political troubles, in which he was plunged as Roman Republican liberties were being extinguished, did not quench his spirit. He was acid at the expense both of Pompey, whom he supported, and Julius Caesar, whom he opposed. When Pompey gave Roman citizenship to a Gaul, Cicero said: 'He is a funny fellow, he gives foreigners a new country, but he cannot give us back our own.' When Pompey asked him where Dolabella, his son-in-law, was in the struggle against Caesar, whose daughter Julia was Pompey's wife, Cicero's quick reply was 'with your father-in-law'. Pompey did not appreciate these smart cracks. In the same spirit, upon encountering a man from Laodicea who had been sent as ambassador to Caesar to beg him to restore liberty to their country, Cicero said to him: 'If you succeed, try to get the same thing for us.' Far from resenting all his sallies, Caesar used to like to hear them, and many a dinner table would have given them a wide circulation.

In the early days of the Empire, not all Romans had learned to be abject slaves. Dining with a merchant Toronius Flaccus, Augustus was so pleased with the music provided by his slaves that he gave them a measure of wheat instead of the money he normally gave on such occasions. When shortly afterwards he asked Toronius to lend him these slaves he got the answer: 'They are at the mill.'

His frivolous daughter Julia was renowned for her wit. Reproached by her father for attending a gladiatorial show surrounded by gay young sparks, while her step-mother Livia was accompanied by grave people of her own age, she replied: 'They will be old too, when I am.' She was, however, fated not to see that day (p. 62). Many of the repartees recorded about her and about other Romans would now be risky even as smoking-room stories. So were the lewd, outspoken remarks of the common people. Soldiers accompanying their victorious general in a Roman triumph, guests at weddings and funerals seemed to think the occasion demanded some exceedingly vulgar, fruity sallies, the lewder, the better. Julius Caesar's legionaries shouted, among other derogatory remarks about their triumphant chief:

'Citizens! keep an eye on your wives, we are bringing a bald old lady-killer.'

The Emperor Tiberius Claudius Nero was hailed as Biberius Caldius Mero, 'the drunkard, wine-flushed, boozer'. 'Tiberius to the Tiber' was another punning form of welcome. It is impossible in a short space to give many examples of the shrewd sallies by Romans of all classes against their rulers and against each other. As it has been said of some similar modern jokes, they are like good mustard which you praise with tears in your eyes.

When the conversation at the dinner table turned upon general topics such as remedies for diseases, the habits of animals, the ways of other countries, the marvels of nature and so forth, it would often seem so strange and so weird that, if we could have overheard it, we might have thought that the assembled company must have come from a lunatic asylum. For the ideas which the Romans exchanged were those of an age before science. Scientific methods, the accurate relation of cause-and-effect in the world of nature, as we know them, had hardly been glimpsed, except perhaps in flashes of intuition by some who were very well versed in Greek literature and by one or two very exceptional people. Few at a fashionable dinner party would read very widely or very critically, and none at all would be likely to know about, still less to undertake, any experiments or research to confirm or deny the extraordinary notions that would be aired in all seriousness by some of the wiseacres reclining in threes round the tables.

At the height of the Roman Empire, long after the Greeks had discovered that the earth is round, the notion could still be contradicted in Rome. 'How was it possible', it would be asked, 'for two men to be the right side up if they had their feet in opposite directions, one on one side of the sphere and the other on the other side?' Questions might also be asked such as 'Why does flesh decay quicker in moonlight than in sunlight?' or 'Have you heard that a man often passing under dewy trees gets leprosy, if he touches the wood?'

On hearing that a friend of one of the guests had jaundice he might be told that he would be cured if he would gaze steadily at a curlew. The fund of stories about the magic of stones, herbs and animals was inexhaustible. There was supposed to be a stone which let out a noise like a trumpet at the approach of

152

64 Dish   65 Fluted bowl

ROMAN SILVERWARE
OF THE SECOND CENTURY A.D.

66 Jug   67 Mixing bowl

thieves, another that changed colour four times a day but could only be seen by young girls. Another turned black in the hands of a liar.

It would not be easy to distinguish truth from falsehood. The magic herb which was supposed to burst into flames whenever a step-mother was scheming to rid herself of a stepson might sound no more extraordinary than a magic white linen which could not be burnt. But this was asbestos and it will not burn.

'Mice in the house?' 'The ashes of a weasel are what you want' or 'Cook a black chameleon. It will cure toothache too!' 'Stomach ache?' 'Wash your feet and drink the water' or 'Make an oil by cooking foxes and hyenas, some alive, some dead.' When a harassed parent says his infant is teething and keeping him awake, the best medical advice might be 'to rub the child's gums with dog's milk, or, if it's a boy, anoint them with hare's brains'. Other guests might contribute such wisdom as: 'They say a ship moves more slowly if the right foot of a tortoise is aboard', or 'Stags hunt snakes to their holes and suck them out by the power of their breath.' Some pronouncements of magicians and the superstitious on these lines were so far-fetched that the more intelligent Romans, even after much wine, would laugh at them; such as the tales about magic herbs that opened barred doors at a touch, that could dry up rivers and swamps or put hostile armies to flight. The recital of alleged cures for diseases was an inexhaustible topic of conversation as there was no limit to the imaginary cures—'the cure of consumption is to take a wolf's liver in thin wine . . . they say also that the smoke of dried cow-dung inhaled through a reed is good'. So near the Romans came to smoking.

The strange story might continue for pages without half exhausting the record of the crazy ideas that not merely circulated in the best society in Rome, but were solemnly set down in black and white by some of the most intelligent Roman writers such as the Elder Pliny and Galen. So we need not be surprised that they lingered on into the Middle Ages. Even today it would not be so very difficult to find somewhat similar notions still lurking here and there, keeping alive all sorts of superstitions about lucky and unlucky days, numbers, stones, plants and practices connected with ladders, new moons and other objects, not to mention all the astrological lore which Cicero, Lucian

153

68 The *triclinium* of the Palace of Domitian, built on the Palatine in A.D. 85

and others without the benefit of any scientific training were easily able to see was utter nonsense two thousand years ago.

The games, chariot races, theatrical shows and pantomimes would also be discussed and the wealthier hosts would probably succeed in getting some of the more famous actors to join the feast. Others might have a miniature pantomime performed as a kind of 'floor-show' to vary the displays by naked dancing girls and there was of course the music.

The talk on some subjects, particularly sex, would strike us as outspoken and frank; and modern psychologists who lay the blame for so many social ills upon 'repression', particularly in sexual matters, would have a hard task to explain why the unrepressed Romans made such a mess of their lives. Long after the meal was over, the guests remained on their couches drinking, so that the guests and the host would usually be in an advanced state of intoxication before the evening was out. The great problem on such occasions was how to delay drunkenness. It has been plausibly suggested that the, to us, revolting habit of vomiting, often on the dining-room floor, in the course of such an evening's entertainment was above all a device to prolong the feast and to avoid drunkenness at the same time.

Political and social tension was unlikely to be so evident among the rich, trading and commercial classes. Their extravagance on a scale in which the well-bred would not be likely to indulge was given free scope, uncontrolled by refined taste or measured restraint. The sort of thing that might happen on such occasions in the first century A.D. has been described in all its

69 Silver cup   70 Drinking horns

DRINKING VESSELS OF THE RICH

rich and fruity extravagance in a fragment of a realistic novel by Petronius, who had been a boon companion of the Emperor Nero until he was falsely accused of conspiracy and chose suicide to avoid a far worse fate. It is the story of a grand feast given by Trimalchio, a vulgar, self-made man who had emerged by great luck from slavery to freedom and to great wealth. Grotesque caricature as it no doubt was, it is still amusing partly because it is the only extensive account we have of all the details of a Roman feast at any time in the thousand years of Rome's history, and partly because its very extravagance highlights the contrast between what could happen in Rome and what happens today. The upshot of the fantastically luxurious living of the richer Romans is significant, but surely not strange. Prolonged self-indulgence brought on boredom and disgust, until at last it helped to drive men's minds in other directions and contributed no doubt to the intense stirrings of religious interest and enthusiasm increasingly noticeable from the second century A.D. onwards, as will be seen in the following chapter.

THE ELEGANT YOUNGER SET

The contrast between the wealth of the rich and the poverty of the very poor was probably greater in Imperial Rome than it is today in London, New York or even in Paris. Yet to many it seemed a good time to be alive. 'I congratulate myself on not having arrived in the world until the present time,' said Ovid; 'this age suits my tastes.' He had assumed a little too much, for the very free poems on the art of love-making in which he said these words upset Augustus, who wished to restore the purer morals of earlier days. Ovid was sent into exile, to a sort of Roman equivalent of Siberia. But all-powerful as Augustus was, he strove against a tide that had long been running and was now too strong for one man to arrest or divert. What was it that made Augustan Rome so attractive to Ovid and the young men and women for whom he wrote his verses? Was it the great influx of gold and pearls and marble and all the other merchandise which loaded the sea with ships and was the outward visible sign of wealth and magnificence? Not a bit of it! Ovid asked himself that very question, only to reply with precision that it was the care of the body and simple elegance of life that made existence so enjoyable.

He launches out into hints both to the young men about town and the young ladies whose pursuit seems to have been the main purpose in life of the young men about town. He advised the men to appear as natural as possible, glowing with health won by physical exercise on the *Campus Martius* with ball-games, javelin- and discus-throwing and horse-riding and by taking ice-cold baths in the water brought by the *Aqua Virgo* aqueduct or in the river Tiber. They should be simply but elegantly turned-out with a well-adjusted toga, free from any stain or blemish, with well-fitting, well-fastened leather shoes and no speck of rust on their fastenings. Hair and beard must be expertly cut, not artificially curled. A girl should be on her guard against a fellow with rings on his fingers whose hair is shiny with oil and whose toga is woven of the very finest wool. Of course finger-nails must be well-trimmed and clean, nose free from hairs and breath and body free from any disagreeable odours. Ovid did not forget to counsel improvement of the mind through the study of the liberal arts, but only for the severely practical purposes of impressing judges and juries and young ladies. Skill without ostentatious show was his ideal; nothing could be more foolish than to address a girl as though she were a public meeting.

Poetry he recommended to the fair sex, particularly the lyric poets, Sappho, Anacreon, Menander among the Greeks, and Propertius, Tibullus, and of course Virgil's *Aeneid*, 'the greatest masterpiece produced by Latium'. As verse-writing was his own enthusiasm, he put in a modest plea not to be forgotten himself which has certainly had the response for which he hoped. Girls also should learn to dance; ballet-dancers enchanted spectators at the theatres. Girls should learn to play many games; not of course those recommended for young men, but something far less strenuous, with dice, knuckle-bones or chessmen. More important than acquiring skill in this way is learning the art of self-control so as to be a good loser. Ovid wrote as though tears, lamentations, unpleasant accusations, anger, hatred and resentment were liable to ruin many games of skill. For outdoor exercise he recommended girls to stroll in Pompey's arcade, to climb up to the new temples and monuments on the Palatine hill. They should frequent the altars of Isis and especially the theatres and the circus races *(77–8)* for there was the best chance to be seen and admired. The freedom of girls at this time in Ancient Rome seems to have been considerable, though admittedly Ovid was writing about freedwomen and those of less strict upbringing than that no doubt still practised in the dwindling number of the better families.

Before setting out, great care must be taken over personal appearance. By no means all women are beautiful, so they must make the most of their charms. Ovid laid great stress on the arrangement of their hair (*71*), which should not always be in the same style but varied every now and again and suited to each particular shape of face. Some women bleached their hair with German 'soap', others openly went to buy wigs near the temple of Hercules and the Muses in the *Campus Martius*. These were mostly made by depriving slave-girls, often Germans, of their tresses. The choice of the right coloured clothes was another problem. It was a mistake to spend a fortune on Tyrian purple or gold embroidery for there was a great range of colours to be had much more economically. A pale complexion should be sought by using chalk powder and the eyes should be shaded with fine charcoal or saffron. Lees of wine were also used. All these preparations must be private. Nothing was worse than to see a girl cleaning her teeth or at her toilet. She should give out that she is still in bed while all this was going on, with one

71 Women's hair styles

157

exception. She might, if her hair was beautiful, be seen having it combed over her shoulders, but not if she was bad-tempered about it, making the poor hair-dresser girl do it up and undo it several times, scratching the girl's face with her finger-nails or sticking a hair-pin into her arms. Over a hundred years later Juvenal describes similar scenes which testify to the odious side of some Roman women, and illustrate the horrors of slavery. Many hints were given by Ovid, some rather apologetically, saying that of course he need not tell a girl to wash her face every morning or to keep her teeth clean. His advice that she should not laugh immoderately or loudly and should not open her mouth wide, but should learn to talk and sing attractively, was probably more necessary. So, it seems, was the advice common to both sexes that they should never drink wine to the point of losing control of their heads and feet.

All these counsels, obvious as they seem to us, were evidently thought useful and necessary for the rising generation. Ovid's book quickly became popular despite his open disregard of marriage vows and his direct incitement to immorality. Romans did not need his book to help them to devote their time to selfish indulgences, as the fierce indictments of Roman Society a century later by Martial and Juvenal were to show.

DANCES

The ancient Romans frowned heavily upon dancing for fun, but already in the second century B.C., after the second Punic War, both girls and boys were being taught to dance. Around 130 B.C. Scipio Aemilianus reported with indignation: 'I have been taken to these academies where I swear there were more than five hundred children of both sexes dancing with cymbals and striking attitudes that would dishonour the most worthless slave.' Yet he led the Greek-loving 'Scipionic Circle'.

Already in Roman society it was not thought wrong for ladies to dance provided that they did not take it seriously and dance so well that they might be taken for professionals. Roman dancing seems to have been more akin to a performance by a single ballerina, or two or three girls making their own music with a tambourine, than to our crowded ballroom dancing by men and women as partners. But the sterner attitude seems to have persisted, at any rate as far as men were concerned. To

158

characterise anything truly ridiculous, the Romans said that it was 'like dancing in a toga'. Cicero as Consul in 63 B.C., defending the Consul-elect, Licinius Murena, against a charge of bribery, had to deal with the accusation that his client had also been seen dancing. This was a very serious charge indeed, said Cicero, to bring against a consul of the Roman people because, if it were true, it would imply many other vices also since 'hardly anyone who is sober dances, unless by chance he is insane; neither when he is alone nor in any temperate and respectable gathering'.

The wild times of the early Empire made ancient restraints seem out-moded. Ovid, as we have seen, was greatly in favour of dancing, particularly for girls, whose grace of movement added so much to their charm. By his day men and women danced together: 'clasp her waist with your hand and let your foot touch hers' was his advice to a young lover, but Romans never seem to have gone in for dancing as we do today. Old-fashioned Romans continued to view dancing with disfavour, particularly when half-crazed Emperors like Caligula, or exhibitionists like Nero, avid for the applause of the mob, themselves began to hop about to entertain the onlookers. Caligula once summoned three grave senators in the middle of the night. They all thought that their last hour had come. All the Emperor wanted was that they should watch him dance. By the end of the Empire, however, there were signs of a very different attitude. Around A.D. 400, Macrobius could seriously ask: 'Have you ever seen a dancer, woman or man, at any dinner party?' His picture of a new sobriety and restraint in social living among the more refined members of society contrasts sharply with St. Jerome's vigorous denunciation of the worldly and sinful life of the times.

CULTURAL INTERESTS
Music

Dinner parties and displays of dancing during the long evenings called for music, another form of art which the Romans did little to cultivate until fairly late in their history.

The Romans of Republican times were much less sensitive than the Greeks and most of them would cheerfully have written-off music as a waste of time. It would have been un-dignified for a free-born Roman to play an instrument or to sing, but they were prepared to tolerate performances by slaves or professionals in small doses. It is no wonder that Romans of the old school should have been profoundly shocked by the Emperor Nero's 'degrading efforts at singing with a *cithara* after the fashion of the stage', as Tacitus described him. Among the satirical verses circulated in Rome was one recounting how the Persians were twanging their bowstrings while the Emperor twanged his *cithara*. The martial music of brass trumpets was more to their taste. These were both straight (the tuba) and curved (the cornet). There is no Latin word for a drum. Flutes and pipes, tambourines, *tympana*, and cymbals were used in religious processions and ceremonies as in those honouring Isis. The ancient Roman religion of the early Republic had its hymns or chants but their musical character was not at all prominent. Poetry in general was sung, usually to a lyre, and in the later

72 Street musicians and musical instruments

1 Pan-pipe   2 Cymbals   3, 4 Flute   5 Tuba

Empire, as we have seen, hosts and hostesses giving dinner parties would provide sweet music throughout the feast.

Apart from street musicians (72) and some theatrical shows, the religious festivals, the processions at the Games and on great State occasions, Romans had few opportunities to hear good music, for there were none of the organised concerts or musical festivals that are so prominent in Western culture today. The comic songs and tunes heard in the theatres would, however, 'catch on' and be hummed or repeated in much the same way as music-hall songs used to be whistled in the street by errand boys in England long before the invention of the gramophone had spread popular ditties throughout the land. Among the very few mechanical aids which the Romans possessed was, curiously, an organ operated by water power. The invention dated from the latter half of the third century B.C. and it came, as did many of the scientific discoveries of the Greeks, from Alexandria. This is the only form of mechanical music of which we have evidence in ancient Rome, but it was doubtless confined to merely a few rich Romans.

Oratory

Martial was of the same mind as Dr. Johnson. For all his sentimental praise of rustic joys (p.143) he soon got sick of them. After three years back home in Spain, despite his marriage there with a rich lady, he confessed to a friend,

> I miss the audience to which I had grown accustomed in Rome and I feel like an advocate in a foreign court. If there be anything pleasing in my small books it comes from those who listened to me. I feel absolutely stranded now that I lack those penetrating judgments, that fertility of invention, the libraries, the theatres, the social gatherings—all those pleasures from which you learn so much unconsciously and which I fastidiously spurned.

Obviously Rome was the place for anyone who set any store by the life of the mind. A popular diversion was to listen to the men whose ability to speak with force and conviction and whose knowledge of the law was displayed in the arguments before judge and jury in the Forum. A keen sense of the merits of the truly eloquent was acquired in this way during the Republic, making the practical study of oratory much more developed and

73 An orator

better understood than it is today. A good speaker impressed the mob also. 'I had to laugh just now,' wrote Catullus fresh from the Forum in 54 B.C. 'My friend Calvus was accusing Vatinius in splendid fashion when a fellow in the crowd, lifting up his hands in admiration, said "Ye Gods, what an eloquent little blighter".' As Tacitus shrewdly pointed out later on, such occasions 'brought the whole community together *en masse*', so that almost any cold fish of a speaker would be fired by their excited interest. 'A public speaker must have applause.' In Imperial times, however, lawsuits were often heard in small rooms where oratorical talent had no scope. Then also, the greatest stimulus to Republican oratory, the delivery of political speeches in the Senate, had disappeared, with the result that oratorical skill sharply declined from the high level to which it had been raised by Cicero and his contemporaries. 'By the operations of the great Imperial system', said Tacitus, 'a hush has come upon eloquence as indeed it has on the world at large.' Another cause of the decline was that the law got more and more complicated and involved, so that it became almost impossible to combine great legal learning with brilliant advocacy. Nevertheless there was always something going on to attract an audience with some intellectual curiosity and time to spare. The fashion grew, towards the end of the Republic and during the Empire, of attending public lectures where poets read their verses. They do not seem to have been very popular. 'Whenever does a public recitation, few and far between as they are, become news all over the City, let alone throughout the provinces?' asked Tacitus around A.D. 85. 'If, fired by the delights of great fame, you decide to give a recitation', said Juvenal a generation later, complaining about a patron's meanness,

> he will lend you a shabby old house long barred up, with doors able to stand a siege. He does not forget to send freedmen to sit in the back rows and clients to applaud loudly, but not one great man will meet the cost of the benches or pay for the tiers of seats resting on hired beams or for the chairs in the front row which have to be returned after the performance.

Books and Reading

It would be wrong to write off all love of literature as negligible among the very practical-minded Romans in the early days of the Republic on the grounds that, as far as we can judge, none but a small minority was touched by it. The same verdict could be pronounced upon the English in Shakespeare's time. It is probably just as true today in England and the United States where personal expenditure on books is deplorably low. Much use is now made of public libraries, but some existed in Rome also. Even today, public expenditure for cultural as distinct from utilitarian objects, upon art, museums, libraries, civic and historic buildings, public parks and open spaces in many a modern city continues to be disgracefully low in relation to the wealth of modern societies. Private expenditure for cultural ends is similarly meagre. Yet, with a derisory fraction of the vast resources of modern times, the ancient Greeks and Romans managed to create cultural masterpieces that shame our 'affluent societies' today. In Rome, as in Europe before the invention of printing, books were at first very costly and scarce. Every *volumen* or roll (from which we get the word 'volume' for a book) had to be written by hand. The use of papyrus, from which our word paper comes, was a capital invention, 'seeing that all the usages of civilised life', as Pliny the Elder pointed out, 'depend to such a remarkable degree upon the use of paper'. There were many grades of writing-paper on the market in Rome. The best came from the centre of the papyrus pith, and was called *hieratica* because it used to be reserved for sacred books. According to Pliny, an ex-schoolmaster and freedman, Fannius, managed to make first-class paper from the third-grade pith. His papers were sold and known by his name as *Fanniana*. As we know from Catullus, waste-paper was used then as today to provide, as he said, 'loose jackets for mackerel' and for lavatory use also.

Black ink which has remained legible to this day was made from soot, resin, pitch, and octopus-ink. Pliny records that Indian ink was imported in the first century A.D. although he said that he did not know how it was made. He seems to have confused it with the purple dye, indigo. Pens were usually of reed or feathers, cut to a point to make a nib like the goose- and turkey-quills of our not very distant ancestors. Writers needed

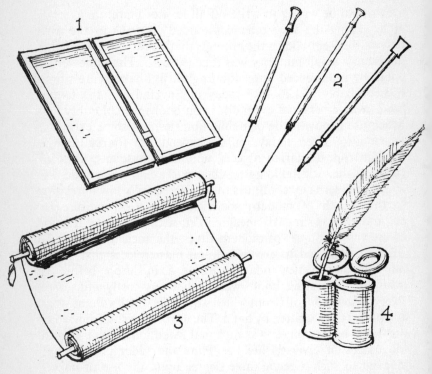

74 Writing equipment

| 1 Wax tablets | 3 Papyrus roll |
| 2 Styli | 4 Ink-wells and quill-pen |

a small quiver full of these indispensable tools of their craft. The *stilus*, a sharp-pointed, thin stick of wood, ivory, reed or metal was used to scratch messages or memoranda upon wax-coated wooden tablets which would be fastened together with cords acting as a kind of hinge. 'A collection of these tablets was called a *caudex* in olden days,' said Seneca. Here is the origin of the word *codex*, used later for a book in pages instead of in a roll.

Usually the roll was written on one side only in columns between 2 and 3 inches in length, with anything from 25 to 45 lines to a column. Normal size handwriting would allow some 18 to 25 letters to a line. Considerable care was given in the better manuscripts to ensure the right proportion of margin at the top and bottom and between the columns. To utilise the back for writing as well was an unsatisfactory economy as the rolls were semi-transparent. School exercises and accounts have, however, been found on the backs of some rolls. A single roll of normal size would contain no more than a book of the Bible of the length of the Gospel of St. Matthew; a long work, such as the complete history of Livy, would have required 142 rolls and was too much for a poor man's library, as Martial complained. Such 'books' must have been physically difficult to consult. A whole roll would have to be unwound to find any desired passage or reference. The papyrus web did not tear as easily as our paper does, but it is difficult to believe that it would have stood up to constant use as well as a book would.

A striking aspect of these ancient rolls, many of which (mostly written in Greek) have been recovered in a good state of preservation from the sands of Egypt, is the difficulty of reading them due to their lack of punctuation marks and to the scribes' habit of joining all the words together without any spaces between them. They began without any title page, which was put at the end of the roll if it was included at all, so that a whole book might need to be unrolled to get at this essential information. As spectacles were unknown in Ancient Rome, ageing scholars had to give up reading as they became less able to focus their eyes upon small script. Many who might have become scholars would never have been able to do so if their eyesight was poor. It was not until the thirteenth century that spectacles began to be used in Europe.

During the Empire leaves of vellum or parchment began to be

used for books as well as paper. The best were made from the skins of calves, lambs and kids by cleaning, scraping and rubbing them smooth and polishing them with chalk.

The new form of a book of folded leaves stitched together, the *codex*, which is our type of book, then began to be made in paper as well as in parchment and for many years the paper *codex* was produced as well as the vellum *codex* and, of course, the papyrus roll. Parchment was very expensive, so books made from it were written in small characters. 'How short a parchment contains the mighty Maro,' said Martial of a copy of the works of Virgil in one volume. Christian authors of the third century A.D. mostly used the *codex*, which stood up better to wear, particularly if made of parchment. It could include much more and was easier of reference than a roll. The four Gospels and the Acts of the Apostles could easily be written in a single *codex*, whereas they would require five separate rolls.

The indifference of the ancient Romans to books is well illustrated by the fact that it was not until the first century B.C. that private libraries became coveted booty of war. Sulla, in 86 B.C. from Athens, and Lucullus, in 67 B.C. from the Near East, returned with valuable collections of books. From this time onwards there is evidence of a keen and growing interest in books. Cicero was an inveterate book-collector. By his time booksellers had begun to open their shops in Rome, some in the Argiletum where Cicero owned property. His passion for books was shared by one or two of his friends, among whom was the learned Pomponius. He earned the name Atticus, by which he is known to history, for his devotion to all things Greek. Shrewd and industrious, he turned his affection into cash dividends by buying well-educated Greek slaves and setting them up as book-copyists. One of them would dictate the text of a book to be copied and a whole band of slave-scribes would write it out. This was the nearest approach the Romans were able to make to the mass-production of books and it seems to have succeeded in making them more abundant and cheaper. The same method of book production was kept up in many monasteries in the Middle Ages.

Slowly, as the years went by, a great number of books had been amassed, and, as many were at first valuable property, a market was developed not in Rome alone but in the provinces of Spain and Gaul. A race of cultivated and knowledgeable booksellers grew up whose shops drew literary men to read the advertisements of new books fixed outside the shops or on the columns of a portico. As books multiplied, so the cost of many of the commoner texts would diminish and many a Roman must have known the excitement of finding a rare volume in a second-hand bookshop.

Cicero has left ample evidence, particularly in his letters, of this absorbing pursuit which added such zest to his life. Never has rhetoric on the subject of books and literature been more finely expressed than in the speech he wrote in support of the appeal of his friend Archias, a poet, for Roman citizenship.

> Unlike all other interests and amusements, which are only suitable at certain special times and places and at particular ages of life, cultural interests and the love of reading are always rewarding: they give power to the young and charm the old; they add grace to prosperity and are a sure refuge and consolation in times of trouble. They delight us at home and never burden our public life. They stand us in good stead through the watches of the night, on our journeys, and in the country.

Conscious that his audience might find this a strange doctrine, he added:

> even if we ourselves are not attracted by such interests, or find them little to our taste, we are in any case bound to respect them in others.

From then onwards no mansion would be complete without its library of shelves or cupboards for collections of many-coloured rolls. Then, as now, rich men with no real literary interests bought libraries for show, only to incur the scorn of philosophers like Seneca, who, himself a millionaire, preached modesty and restraint to others, denouncing those who 'lacking the most elementary culture, possess books not for study but as a decoration for their dining-rooms'. No house of any pretensions, he said, lacked 'its library with shelves of rare cedar wood and ivory from floor to ceiling as well as its hot and cold bathing rooms'. It stirred his bile to see 'the works of divine genius bought merely for show to decorate a wall'. Despite such a lashing, the newly rich continued the practice and thereby kept many an honest bookseller active from whose industry real scholars were also able to benefit.

In Ancient Rome of the Republic, as in England until the eighteenth century was well advanced, there were no public libraries at which books could be readily consulted. During the first years of the new Empire, C. Asinius Pollio, who had helped Augustus on the road to power, devoted his declining years to literature. Before his death at the age of 80, in A.D. 4, he became, according to Pliny, 'the first who, by forming a public library, made the genius of learned men public property'. It was evidently a successful and popular move because Augustus added a library of both Greek and Latin works to the temple of Apollo he had built on the Palatine and another to the portico or arcade he built in memory of his sister Octavia. Succeeding Emperors continued the good work, so that by the second century A.D. there were over 25 public libraries in Rome alone. It was possible to borrow books for home reading in the later centuries of the Empire. There were public libraries in the great public Baths. The troubled days of the later Empire prevented the increase or enlargement of library facilities and literary-minded folk grew less and less until, towards the end of the fourth century A.D., Ammianus Marcellinus sadly records that for lack of readers many libraries were shut and as silent as the grave.

When we ask how far the love of books and the habit of reading spread among the common people, we come up almost against a blank wall of ignorance. The masses left no 'letters or memoirs and very few indications of their reading habits. Curiously, it is from otherwise blank walls that some clues have come. Like many people, the inhabitants of Pompeii used to scrawl on walls and some remains of what they wrote have been discovered as the wrecked city has been cleared of ash and lava. There schoolboys have spelled out some words from Virgil, lovers have remembered what Ovid, Tibullus and Propertius wrote in moods of tender passion. Verses predominate, although the Roman poets never wrote in easily remembered rhyme. Many of all these scribblings may have been from school memories, for boys and girls were made to read the renowned authors of Rome, such as Plautus and Terence, as well as the more voluminous works of dramatists such as Caecilius, Afranius, Pacuvius, Accius and others, none of whose works have come down to us. They may not have read the love poems of

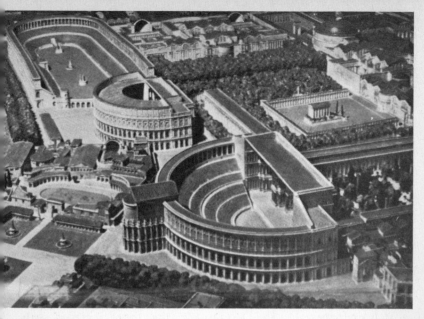

75 The Theatre of Pompey, Rome's first stone theatre, built in 55 B.C. and able to seat 40,000 spectators. Behind are the Odeon (another theatre) and Stadium of Domitian, and, to the right, the Baths of Nero and Agrippa

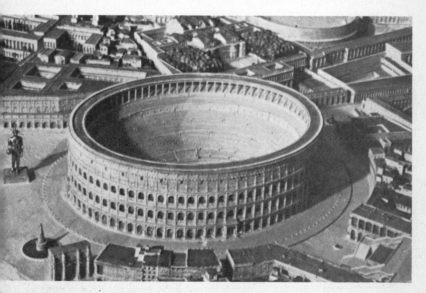

76 The Colosseum, the amphitheatre of the Flavians, which had a seating capacity of 50,000. The statue on the left is the Colossus of Nero

Catullus, Propertius, Tibullus and Ovid at school, but extracts from their poems appear on the walls.

From the fact that there were between 20 and 30 public libraries in Rome during the Empire, as well as an active book-selling trade, we may conclude that perhaps the average Roman during the Empire did not after all lag so very far behind the average American or Britisher in the interest he or she took in books and reading. From quite early days during the Republic, Cicero made it clear that the Roman crowd was by no means lacking in literary discrimination. 'They at once notice faulty rhythm', he said, 'and appreciate a well-turned phrase, or a sublime thought.' When for the first time in 163 B.C. the famous line of Terence, *homo sum: nihil humanum a me alienum puto*, was spoken in the theatre the audience rose in frenzied applause. They were also prepared to reverence true talent. It is recorded that, when the poet Virgil entered to take his seat in the theatre, everyone stood up as one man. On the whole, however, subtleties, the finer emotions, the more carefully chosen and ripely matured thought and expression, the more wide-reaching allusions escaped them. Vast masses, particularly in the country, remained untouched by literary interests. To give a book to a country dweller could be cited by Seneca as an example of a silly present.

SHOWS AND SPECTACLES

The average Roman did not lack entertainment and amusement, indeed the great attraction of the City was the endless succession of things to see. Idle Romans were catered for by travelling performers of every sort at street corners and in public places. Conjurors, clowns, jugglers, fortune-tellers, snake-charmers were always going their rounds, endeavouring to pick up a few small coins or some other reward from the idle crowds who thronged the streets, markets, gardens and porticos of the vast Imperial City.

They would compete with all kinds of beggars, including pavement artists and singers among whom would probably be one of those ship-wrecked mariners who, having lost his ship and its cargo, was reduced, as Juvenal said, to 'a rag to cover his cold and nakedness and a poor morsel of food while he begs for pennies and supports himself by a painting of a storm'.

169

77 The *Circus Maximus* the largest and most magnificent of the Roman circuses. Rebuilt by Julius Caesar and restored by Augustus, it was enriched by later emperors, such as Vespasian, Titus and Hadrian. It seated 250,000 spectators (Strahov Stadium, Prague with 240,000 seats is today the world's greatest)

'Shall I be touched and produce a penny', Persius asks, 'if a ship-wrecked sailor sings a song, carrying on his shoulder a picture of himself on a broken plank?' All these diversions were very amateur paltry amusements compared with the great thrills publicly provided, free of charge, in theatres, amphitheatres and great race-tracks.

'Bread and the games in the circus,' said the poet Juvenal with withering contempt at the beginning of the second century A.D., were the only things that the average Roman city-dweller worried about. Like all bitter satirists, he exaggerated. The Roman mobs liked milling about in the Forum and market places, jostling in the narrow streets, looking at processions, watching street performers, listening to ranting lawyers and joining in the stream of life as it flowed on day by day. They enjoyed their afternoons at the great Baths and relished a cup of hot wine and water, a snack and a gossip in a small wine or cook-shop, when they could afford it, to supplement their ration of free corn and any scraps they were able to pick up from a rich man's house. But in the main Juvenal was right. The rage for great public spectacles by his time had become a mania. Musical and athletic shows and theatrical plays on Greek lines held some place among them, but the raw taste of the masses craved for stronger stimulants, as the fate of the Roman theatre shows.

The Stage

Organised entertainments developed rather slowly in the first three centuries of the Republic. Theatrical shows, which were an everyday affair among Rome's Greek and Etruscan neighbours, began to be put on in temporary theatres after Roman soldiers had spent 20 years in Sicily during their first war with the Phoenicians. The Island was then divided between the Carthaginians and the Greeks. After some defeats, the Greeks joined the Romans, and the Roman legionaries encountered, for the first time, a new form of art in the tragedies of Euripides and the comedies of Menander. In the first year of peace (240 B.C.) a play in Latin was performed in Rome which whetted the public taste for more. Within the next 150 years almost all the comedies and tragedies of Roman literature had been written. But, before the end of the Republic, the theatre as a form of art was dead. It was not that the comedies of Plautus, Terence, the tragedies of Ennius, Naevius, Pacuvius, Accius or the later tragedies of Seneca, imitated as most of them were from Greek originals, lacked merit or were unappreciated. They simply could not compete with the rival forms of entertainment which made a stronger appeal to the Roman mob. Mimes, pantomimes and knockabout farces still drew crowds to the theatres, but, throughout the Empire, mention of 'The Games' (*ludi*), which included theatrical entertainments, meant for most people the exciting chariot races in the *Circus Maximus*, and above all the bloody gladiatorial combats in the amphitheatres.

Chariot Races

Chariot races were immensely popular and although very dangerous they lacked the intentional brutality of the man-and-beast fights. They took place in one of the five or six circuses in Imperial Rome of which the biggest and the oldest was the great *Circus Maximus*(77), which was 600 yards long and 200 yards in width, able to hold, after it had been enlarged during the Empire, a quarter of a million spectators. Most of them sat on wooden seats built up behind the front rows, which were of stone and reserved for Vestal Virgins, senators and knights. More than once restored and rebuilt, and adorned with marble and gilded statues, it was one of the most magnificent of the many sights of Rome. Four teams owned by contractors competed for popular favour, the reds, the greens, the whites and the blues, so called from the colours of the drivers standing in the slight two-wheeled chariots behind two or four horses(78), the reins round their bodies. They had to cut themselves free quickly if they were upset. Passions aroused in favour of one or other of these colours could divide families and wreck friendships. Men, women and children began to pour into the Circus before dawn. Late-comers could not find a place free unless they had hired some poor man to reserve them a seat. No man was admitted unless in a toga, the badge of citizenship, so slaves were excluded. The sound of an approaching band heralded the entry of the presiding consul in his chariot with his impressive retinue of lictors, attendants, legionaries and cavalry followed by the performers, the many teams of chariots. Singers and priests, followed by incense-bearers carrying gold and silver censers, led in the images of gods and goddesses borne aloft on biers or

78 A four-horse chariot rounding one of the turning-posts in the Circus

riding in chariots, all of whom received tremendous applause.
The appearance of the Emperor in his grand lodge or box was
the signal for renewed cheers.

When the Consul dropped a white handkerchief the first four
teams rushed out to begin the first heat, or *missus*. Each was
seven laps, or about six miles. A normal day would see 10 or 12
such heats, but later in the Empire as many races as could be
crowded in from sunrise to sunset were run under the hot Italian
sun.

The charioteers were usually slaves or men of low class, and
none but the skilful and the lucky survived. The memorial of
one of the more famous, Diocles (*c.* A.D. 150), records his 3,000
victories in a two-horse chariot and 1,462 with more than two
horses. Before he retired at the age of 42 he had beaten veterans,
some who had won more victories than he had. One such
charioteer won 50 purses of gold in an hour, and yet another, a
North African, between A.D. 115 and 129 gained over a million
and a half sesterces.

There were race-cards and placards advertising the horses and
their drivers, for betting, often for great stakes, was general.
The poet Martial was indignant that his name was unknown

while that of a favourite chariot horse would be on everybody's lips and the drivers the darlings of society.

Before the building of the first amphitheatre in the reign of Augustus, the *Circus Maximus* was used for fights to the death between gladiators and for wild-beast hunts, both entertainments which rivalled, if they did not eclipse, the chariot-races as popular entertainments.

A Day at the Amphitheatre

In the year A.D. 80 the great oval amphitheatre, now known as the Colosseum(76), was inaugurated by the Emperor Titus with the most lavish Games. They were advertised to last one hundred days. Fights to the death between more than 10,000 prisoners and 5,000 wild animals were promised. On the second day there were to be horse races and on the third day a naval battle between 3,000 men on an artificial lake made by flooding the arena. No full record of what actually happened has been preserved, but we may follow, in its main outlines at least, an imaginative reconstruction of the scene by a French writer.

On the opening day enormous crowds poured down all the streets and alleys, pushing, shoving and scrambling to fill the top half of the immense number of seats looking down on the huge arena. The whole of Rome was there. The first rows were filled with senators, priests, augurs, magistrates and other officials of distinction. The Vestal Virgins had a special place of honour opposite the Imperial box or lodge. Up to the first 17 rows were crammed with worthy citizens of wealth and standing. Above them and entirely filling the second and third rows up to the very top was the mob making up the great mass of the inhabitants of the Imperial City. It was their show, for the whole amphitheatre and the lavish shows held in it were arranged to keep them amused. Excitable, noisy, their near-animal instincts and passions unrestrained by education, good manners or breeding, they were squashed promiscuously together, men, women and children, crying, shouting, sweating in a deafening crescendo of noise under the great spread of canvas which sailors of the fleet had slung as a partial roof from masts all round the amphitheatre's rim, to serve as a shield against the sun. It made a hothouse of the upper seats. After the solemn, long procession of civic dignitaries, priests and performers,

173

together with images of the gods, the entry of the Emperor Titus across the floor of the arena was the signal for renewed frenzied applause from the restive crowd. A tremendous fanfare of trumpets followed. The Games began. A rough-and-tumble pantomime-show, followed by some incredibly clever conjurers, made very little impression. Their skill was lost on the great crowds, most of whom were too high up to see what was going on in any detail. More impressive were 12 four-horse teams of circus riders, each man standing astride a pair of horses driving another pair yoked in front, racing madly round each other and round the arena. Neither they nor the show of performing animals which followed, excited much enthusiasm. The audience began to get impatient. Quickly these preliminaries were ended. It was the turn of the gladiators, men trained for battle, sworn to the gladiators' oath to suffer death by fire, in chains, under the lash or by the sword as their master might decide and to obey as a true gladiator should.

A shrill fanfare of trumpets announced the entry of two teams of 24 gladiators in charge of two renowned trainers, themselves former gladiators who, scarred and maimed, had somehow survived with their glory from many a combat. According to tradition, 24 men heavily armed as the ancient Samnites, Rome's oldest enemies, faced 24 lightly clad and lightly armed 'Thracians', each with exposed chests, a small round shield and a sharp curved dagger, as fatal as a wild boar's tusk. As befitted such a tremendous occasion, all the gladiators' leg-shields, metal helmets and armaments were most ornate and brightly polished(79). Both teams marched smartly up to face the Emperor in his resplendent Imperial Box to shout as one man: 'Hail, Caesar. Those about to die salute you.'

The first encounter was a mere joust with blunt weapons, but this was not suffered to last long. The crowd yelled for a fight to the finish *sine missione*. New swords and daggers with fine, keen cutting edges were brought in and some were presented to the Emperor so that there was no doubt about their sharpness. The serious business then began. Flashing swords, the clash of steel, and the first wounds aroused the passions, the hatred and the desperate fury of the gladiators and inflamed the blood-lust of the mob. The shouts and yells and screams of the onlookers grew to a huge, roaring crescendo of sound as one Samnite after

174

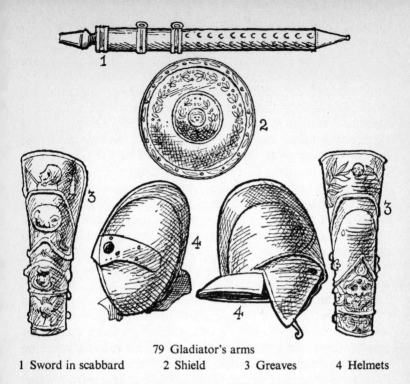

79 Gladiator's arms

1 Sword in scabbard	2 Shield	3 Greaves	4 Helmets

another went down with their stomachs gashed open or their necks spouting blood and one Thracian after another crumpled with a Samnite sword through his chest. Reinforcements were rushed in to restore the balance and to add to the pile of bleeding, writhing bodies on the sand-strewn floor. At last this sort of fighting seemed to have gone on long enough to satisfy, momentarily, the mob. The few survivors retired to get their laurel crowns, their bags of gold and to anticipate the adulation of Rome. Squads of little men ran into the arena with ropes and metal hooks to drag the bodies of the dead and wounded to a mortuary cell where valuable weapons and armour were retrieved and sorted out. The gasping, bleeding, groaning wounded were finished off, for nobody had any use for a maimed gladiator who, if nursed back to health, might never fight again. The bodies were then piled into carts to be taken and flung into a nameless common grave.

Meanwhile bands of slaves were spreading fresh sand over

the blood-drenched battleground, called an arena from the Latin word for sand, *harena*. Two famous gladiators on horseback then galloped in, to the frenzied applause of their fans. Both had been victors in many fights; both were idols of the mob. They put up a show which made the crowd delirious until one of the horses was brought down, terribly gashed. Its rider, rolling on the sand, was quickly mastered before he could rise. With a foot on his neck as he lay prostrate, his opponent held his sword aloft. Was the vanquished man to live or die? The crowd had slaked its first lust for blood on the Samnites and Thracians. The Vestal Virgins and the Emperor raised their hands and their signal for mercy was generally followed, so the two heroes lived to fight another day. As they left the arena, the wretched horse, writhing in agony, was dragged away, leaving dark trails of blood in the sand.

A great novelty followed. Ostriches and giraffes, which few Romans had seen before, were released after a long captivity. Scenting fresh air and enjoying a new-found liberty, they sought to get back the use of their legs and to run joyously round the arena, to the vast amusement of the crowd. It was a short-lived respite. Bands of archers ran into the arena and the slaughter began. Wounded and startled animals fled in all directions as the arrows hissed and struck, vainly seeking an escape from which the pitiless high walls of the arena barred them. It was soon strewn with the dead and the dying. The hooks and the ropes were busy for some time removing them to make room for two elephants whose tusks had been fitted with long, sharp iron spikes. Driven to fight, a desperate battle ensued amid the thunder of hooves and the tremendous trumpetings of the enraged beasts. At length one managed to tear open the belly of his opponent and so to finish the fray. The slaves below were still working desperately to clear off the dead giraffes and ostriches, so a criminal was brought in to be left to the victorious elephant to execute. Sick with fear and paralysed by the knowledge that he had no escape, with the eyes of Rome upon him, the wretched man flung himself down as though in hope that the elephant might have pity on him. Still enraged, panting and trumpeting after his tremendous battle, the great beast soon saw him and it was not long before a great foot cracked his skull as though it had been a nut. It then remained to finish

176

80 The Colosseum: duel between a *retiarius* and a *mirmillo*

off the victorious elephant. After the archers had come back to madden the great brute with hundreds of arrows which stuck like huge darts into its hide while it was trying madly to avenge itself, with blood pouring from a hundred wounds, the show seemed likely to go on too long for the patience of the crowds, so a quick lance thrust into a vulnerable spot managed to bring it to an end. To drag off two dead elephants was at first beyond the strength of the attendants and their ropes and hooks. Teams of dray horses had quickly to be found while the impatient mob hissed, whistled and shouted abuse, yelling for more gladiators.

Six *retiarii*, provided with nothing but a sharp, spiked trident and a net, were brought in to face an equal number of *mirmillones*, so called from the fish ornament on their helmets, armed with a short, thick sword, an oblong shield and leg and arm shields of metal. Those who became enmeshed in the skilfully thrown net were soon left bleeding to death from many wounds, but some swordsmen claimed an easy victim when a net went awry. After breathless encounters, to the delirious joy of the onlookers, one slender figure alone remained among the swordsmen, and one *retiarius* (*80*), a great gorilla of a man, all muscle and no forehead, the darling of the mob, the pride and joy of Rome, hero of a hundred fights whose uncanny skill with the net seemed to guarantee invincibility. The lone *mirmillo* leaned on his sword as though in disdain and disgust. To refuse to fight was unforgivable and cries of 'coward' were raised. Goaded to action, he sprang to the attack with such skill that time after time the net was parried and at last the vaunted champion was at his mercy, rolling in the sand and begging the mob to spare his life. The novel and unexpected turn the battle had taken was too much for the crowd, which knew no mercy. It was just as ready to make a hero out of the newcomer who, when his helmet was raised, was seen to be a fair-haired and very handsome Gaul. Hands began to turn down; more and more. There could be no doubt about the verdict. It called for a quick thrust, leaving one more corpse to be dragged away with the rest, and with them a legendary hero vanished from the Roman scene.

The afternoon was wearing on. Could the thrills be kept up any longer? Barred doors were opened and two or three hundred wretched, ill-clad creatures of all ages were driven into the centre of the arena as the doors closed behind them.

'Jews! Jews! Death to the Jews!', bawled the mob. They were prisoners brought back by Titus from the Jewish war and the destruction of Jerusalem. As slaves, they had been forced to exhaust themselves helping to finish building that very amphitheatre in which they were to die. As the mob screamed, howled and roared, more barred doors were lifted, releasing man-eating lions and tigers who had not been fed for quite a time. They bounded forth to rush upon easy, unarmed prey.

The light was beginning to fade and to cast longer shadows over the arena before the long work of clearing it could begin. The crowd was already leaving while mounds of corpses were being removed, so that armies of slaves could begin to make everything ready for the slaughter of a new day. For this one day was merely the beginning. Throughout 14 more consecutive weeks thereafter the slaughter was to continue to make one of the most renowned holidays Romans could remember. So it went on year by year throughout the centuries, to provide a succession of scenes of brutality and bloodshed of which the Romans and the immigrant adopted Romans of slave stock seem never to have tired.

ROMAN DYNAMISM

Everyday life in the Imperial City of Rome evidently had a very seamy, revolting side. But while the lazy mob and leisured folk were finding amusement there in these and other sordid ways, very many active and energetic men were running a vast empire and pushing ahead with the great work of consolidating and extending the Roman hold on the rest of the world.

During the fifty years following the lurid inauguration of the blood-stained Colosseum, the Roman Empire was to expand yet further. The boundary line along the Rhine and Danube, the *limes*, was established and fortified, and then Hadrian set up a wall and a line of fortifications in Britain from the Tyne to the Solway. Vast building plans were started all over the Empire which was also kept busy by increasing trade and development. Roman dynamism made the business life of the cities hum with an activity upon which the degenerate idle proletariat, in the queues for free bread and circuses, were mere parasites. Yet, relatively insignificant as they then were, they seem in relation to later developments to be both a symbol and a portent of something rotten at the core of an otherwise virile and dynamic society.

Chapter VII

RELIGION

'WE Romans', said Cicero, 'owe our supremacy over all other peoples to our piety and religious observances and to our wisdom in believing that the spirit of the gods rules and directs everything.' Roman rites and observances took two main forms. One was the domestic reverence of the spirit or *genius* of the family, and particularly of its head, and of its hearth and home. The other was the public attitude to the gods and goddesses by whom the destiny and welfare of the Roman people as a whole were supposed to be guided and controlled. Jupiter, Mars, Apollo, Mercury and Neptune were the chief gods; Juno, Vesta, Minerva, Ceres, Diana and Venus were the principal goddesses. Temples, priests and sacred rites were provided by the State for the special task of interceding with them. The ordinary Roman man or woman had little personal part to play in such rites. While they were being undertaken and fulfilled it was the duty of the ordinary citizen not to interfere or make any disturbance and to refrain from any business affairs.

Romans kept their religious faith because they grew up with it in their homes. Its strength did not depend so much upon visits to the temples or upon the services of the priests because every home, however poor, had its domestic shrine and altar before which a daily act of reverence took place. These shrines and the little statuette on them of the *Lar familiaris*(13), the guardian spirit of the home, have been mentioned already in Chapter II because they were part of Roman family life. There were *lares* of the cross-roads also, who could be worshipped out of doors and by the homeless or by those too poor to maintain their own family shrine. 'In the City', said Ovid, 'there are a thousand Lares', and they were worshipped with the image dedicated to the Genius of Augustus, the first Emperor who did much to restore old religious practices. The City itself had its

180

own *Lares*, 'the twins who guard the cross-road and ever keep watch in our City', as Ovid described them. Their ancient altar (*81*), rebuilt by Augustus, was on the way up the *Via Sacra* to the Palatine hill. Its foundations near the Arch of Titus are still to be seen and an inscription to the *Lares Publici* was found there. The City of Rome also had its own *Penates*, housed in a little chapel on the Velia.

81 Altar of Augustus and the Lares

STATE RELIGION

Gods and goddesses were supposed by the Greeks to reside on the top of Mount Olympus because, although under 10,000 feet, it was the highest peak in the Greek Peninsula. The Romans took over this belief in early times and kept it alive. But by the end of the Republic and in the early days of the Roman Empire few educated Romans seemed to have retained any genuine belief in the existence of the gods. If the poet Ovid is a fair sample, they thought it a good thing to keep the popular beliefs alive: 'It's useful that there should be gods', he said, 'so let's believe there are, and let incense and wine be brought to their ancient shrines.' These gods and goddesses dwelt in temples, where they would be represented in the form of a statue, which in Rome's early days might be a crude wooden figure but later an exquisite work of art in marble, painted in colour and adorned with gold, silver and priceless gems.

Temple worship was no essential part of Roman life. If it had been, it is difficult to understand why Augustus should have had to repair 82 of them which were said to have 'collapsed through age or to have been destroyed by fire'. There were not more than about a hundred within the City confines, which is no great number in a city of some million inhabitants. As buildings they were essentially simple in plan. Some were quite small, while the largest usually contained merely a long room

181

housing a statue (sometimes very large) of a god or goddess (*56*), under an arched roof which was supported upon rows of tall columns of stone or marble flanking the inner room, or sanctuary, on all sides. The elegance of the Corinthian columns, the sculptured ornamentation round the frieze and on the entablature over the entrance (all of which were coloured or gilded), the sculptured horse-drawn chariots of the gods and goddesses on the four corners and apex of the roofs, the marble entrance stairs, all contrived to give them a grave, resplendent and impressive appearance (*1*).

What went on inside the temples? On this interesting question very little information exists and what we can glean relates as much to the secular purposes they served as to their religious use. From a very early time the temples had housed the State Treasury. Julius Caesar, after he had seized the power of the State, had to threaten to kill the Temple guards before he was able to lay his hands upon the public treasury. The temples were also national museums of art and sculpture, for many of the works of the most renowned Greek artists which had been brought to Rome as trophies or as war-loot were placed in the temples. The whole of Greece was ransacked for valuable artistic objects, so Rome must have been a precious storehouse of marvellous jewellery, embroideries, furniture, cups, vases, gold and silver ware, bronzes, statues and pictures, representing every period of Greek art. If the Elder Pliny was right, it seems that few Romans had the time to go to look at all these marvels. 'Indeed,' he said, 'at Rome there is a multitude of works of art, but beautiful as they are, they tend to be forgotten because of their great number and the claims of business and other duties, for great quiet and leisure are necessary in order to admire them fully.'

Private people were also allowed to deposit gold and silver and money in the temples, where they were stored in cellars. This is why one of the first acts of a victorious invading enemy was to loot the temples of their defeated victims.

The Roman Senate frequently met in a temple since it could not lawfully transact public business except in a rectangular building which had been formally 'inaugurated' by the augurs. Seats or benches must therefore have been provided. It would seem that the temples must have been furnished in some such way, and that their roof beams were of wood, otherwise it is difficult to imagine how they could have been destroyed by fire, as several are known to have been, including the great temple of Jupiter Capitolinus. Nothing in the nature of religious services as we know them, in which the body of worshippers as a whole were able to participate, seems to have been celebrated in the temples. Any set forms of prayers, hymns or chants were performed solely by the official priests whose secrets they remained. Many such ceremonies, like that of taking the auspices and offering sacrifices to the gods (*1, 82*), were mostly performed outside the temples on some special shrines or altars. As important as the priests were the 16 augurs whose duty it was to tell from signs in the sky whether the gods liked or disliked some proposed action. The signs came either from the flight of birds, from thunder or from the way sacred chickens ate their food. These augurs were an older 'college' (meaning persons filling any office along with others) than the *haruspices*, who were supposed also to be able to interpret supernatural signs by examining vital organs such as the livers of animals sacrificed by the priest. This was a bit of mystery-mongering which the Romans took over from the Etruscans. It lasted well into the Christian era. Neither the augurs nor the *haruspices* could practice their magic unless asked to do so by the presiding civil magistrate.

When religiously minded Romans dropped into a temple in order to worship the god or goddess whose house it was, they

82 Animals being led to sacrifice

usually had some practical object in view; some personal favour or advantage. They came and perhaps burnt incense. When praying they stood with upturned palms. Sometimes they got as near to the image of the god as they could in order to whisper their pleas; the feet of some images were worn by the kisses of generations of devout worshippers.

A fairly common practice, especially if they were making some unusual petition such as to be cured of some serious malady, was for people to spend a night in the temple. Tablets have been recovered from the ruins of temples and sanctuaries recording thanksgiving for cures of all kinds. In addition to paying a fee for admission, the grateful petitioner for divine aid also brought sacrifices and thank offerings to the temples. Enormous numbers of livestock and cattle, large donations and benefactions and other pious gifts went to augment the wealth of the temples, and to swell the incomes of the priests and attendants, many of whom became rich. The scepticism of sophisticated writers and the aloof attitude of many of the leaders of society to these popular manifestations of religious zeal must not blind us to the fact, supported by the evidence of countless inscriptions, that, despite the allurements of a welter of competing faiths, religions and superstitions, very many Romans down to the second and third centuries A.D. still retained much of the religious zeal of their forefathers.

FESTIVALS AND GAMES

In addition to these formal observances in the old-style Roman homes and at the public altars in front of the temples, Roman religious feeling came out strongly in the very large number of public festivals and at the Games. In fact the Games began by being part of the public religious ceremonial of the Roman people, as is indicated by references to the supposed participation in them of the gods and goddesses of the City (p. 171). However, by the time of Martial and of Juvenal, the crowds who thronged the streets, the theatres and the circuses had little knowledge of, or interest in, any ceremonial meaning there might once have been behind the Games; nevertheless the ancient traditions inspiring them were kept alive. The religious feelings behind the Games seem to have been of a special and limited sort, a natural and intense desire to foster and to maintain

Life—the private and individual lives of the worshippers, the life of the Roman people and the bounty and fertility of Nature as well. All these matters were considered to be in the hands of the gods and goddesses, the more powerful of whom had annual festivals dedicated in their honour.

Many of the Romans themselves were ignorant of this early religious aspect of their apparently mundane, secular games and festivals, so it came about that games staged at first to gratify the gods and to do them honour, soon descended to the very low level of gratifying the baser passions of the hungry, ignorant, lazy and idle mob.

The old traditional Roman Year began on March 1st, when the Vestal Virgins relit the sacred fire on Vesta's hearth, and fresh laurels were hung on public buildings. Old primitive preparations for war were kept up, such as dances of the *Salii* and the traditional horse-races and the ceremony of the trumpets of war. In March also there was the ancient festival of Anna Perenna, goddess of the full year. Fascinating glimpses of the common people of Rome celebrating such ancient ceremonies are to be had in what remains of Ovid's poem *Fasti*. Here it is only possible to mention quickly the greater religious festivals in the Roman Calendar. The *Ludi Megalenses* were held between April 4th and 10th. They were in honour of Cybele, the great Mother Goddess, whose image had been brought to Rome amid extraordinary scenes of ecstasy and mass hysteria in 204 B.C.: in that year the processions, fastings, purifications and other religious ceremonies lasted for 12 days. After 191 B.C. the Megalensian Games were held every year. These were closely followed by the *Ludi Ceriales* in honour of Ceres, the ancient corn goddess of Italy, whose festival and games were of the greatest antiquity. These lasted from April 12th to 19th. Flora, the goddess of flowers, was honoured by festivities from April 28th to May 3rd. Her festival was an exceedingly gay carnival: tables were piled with flowers and the people would dance around, crowned with garlands of flowers. According to Ovid, the *Ludi Florales* were 'marked by licentiousness and broader jests'. The Floral Week ended on May 3rd. From then onwards harvesting and work in the fields used to make heavy demands, so the Romans had to wait seven weeks for their next games.

These were held in honour of Apollo. The *Ludi Apollinares*

had been begun at the bidding of an oracle in 212 B.C. Held between July 6th and 13th each year, they were the occasion for wild-beast fights and horse-races in the Circus, and for pantomimes and shows in the theatres. The *Ludi Romani*, the Roman Games, lasting from September 4th to 19th, had their origin in the legendary days of the Roman Kings and were held in honour of Jupiter, the father-god of the Roman people. The last great religious festival in the traditional Roman year to be celebrated by games, was the *Ludi Plebei*. Dating from 220 B.C., these were held between November 4th and 17th. Alone among the great public festivals they had had no particular religious origin but like the Roman Games, were made the occasion for a great feast in honour of Jupiter.

Of all the December festivals the *Saturnalia* is the most renowned. Held originally as a one-day feast on the 17th of the month, when the autumn sowing would be over, it grew until it occupied seven days. Reduced to three by Augustus, it was later extended to five. All Rome, according to Seneca, went mad. The ceremonies began soberly enough as the toga-clad senior Romans attended the public sacrifice in Saturn's temple by the Forum. Then followed a feast at which togas were discarded for tunics or, for those who possessed one, the gayer dinner gown, the *synthesis*. On the following days no *Saturnalia* was complete without the sacrifice of a suckling pig, just as an English Christmas demands a turkey or roast

83 A priest

186

beef and plum-pudding. Household slaves were waited on by their masters as though the Golden Age had returned when all men were free, but the Lord of Misrule appointed to preside over the feast as a kind of mock-king may have been a reminder that during the *Saturnalia* everything was turned upside down.

If the poet Martial was a typical Roman city-dweller, it is plain that hopes for valuable presents from the rich ran high 'in December's month, when napkins fly about and slender spoons, wax-tapers and paper and pointed jars of dried damsons'. Pickled fish, sausages, beans, olives, figs, prunes, nuts, cheap wine were also very usual gifts, but Martial, who could be a shameless beggar at times, makes it clear that what he always hoped for was something much more valuable, such as a gift of silver dishes and antique goblets. Yet despite all his scorn of those who gave him little when he was hoping for much, he had learned one great truth which it is surprising to read from a Roman's hand: 'The only wealth you keep for ever is that which you give away' (*quas dederis solas semper habebis opes*).

In January and February the Romans kept up several traditional religious observances, such as that in honour of Janus, guardian spirit of entrances to towns and homes and the god presiding over the beginnings of all things and all deeds. In the old religious days he was worshipped at the beginning of each day, each month and each year. His name survives in the word January. In this month also the fortune-telling goddess Carmenta was honoured on January 11th and 15th.

February for the founding fathers of the Roman Republic was a busy month in the fields, yet time was spared for several religious festivals that seem to have had little direct relation to the labours on the land. February 21st was a public holiday on which, as on All-Souls day in Catholic countries, remembrance and honour were given to the dead. 'Appease the souls of your fathers', said Ovid on this day:

> The ghosts ask for but little: they value piety more than a costly gift . . . a tile wreathed with votive garlands, a sprinkling of corn, a few grains of salt, bread soaked in wine and some loose violets; these are enough. Put them on a potsherd and leave it in the middle of the road.

These rites were the culmination of ceremonies which had begun on February 13th and they were followed immediately by a family re-union on February 22nd, the *Caristia*. Named from the dear (*cari*) loving kinsfolk so meeting together, it followed very naturally upon the ceremonies honouring their ancestors. 'Sweet it is no doubt', sang Ovid, 'after so many lost, to look upon those of our blood who are left.' It was the day to forget and forgive, to patch up quarrels and to reassert family unity in the presence of the household gods, the *Lares*, who shared in the sacred meal.

During the annual ceremonies in honour of the dead, on February 15th, another strange observance took place in Rome at the cave called the *Lupercal*. This was at the foot of the steep Palatine hill on the south-west side, the traditional spot where the she-wolf was supposed to have acted as a foster-mother to Romulus and Remus, the founders of Rome. Year after year, from time immemorial down to the latest days of Christian Rome, at the festival of *Lupercalia*, held on that day, a dog and some goats were sacrificed and sacred cakes were offered which had been made by the Vestal Virgins from ears of corn of the previous harvest. Two youths of noble birth then had their foreheads smeared with blood from the knife used in the sacrifices and this was wiped off with wool dipped in milk. Then they had to laugh. Wrapped in the skins of the slaughtered goats they had a magnificent meal, after which they had to run with two companies each led by one of them, round the base of the Palatine Hill. As they did so they had to strike at all the women they met with strips of skin cut from the hides of the sacrificed goats. These strips were called *februa* (that which purifies) and our month February comes from the same word.

The *Quirinalia* honouring Romulus, Rome's founder; the *Terminalia*, festival of the god of boundaries; the *Regifugium* commemorating, as the Romans thought, the flight of their last Etruscan King, Tarquin, and the *Equirria* on February 27th, a horse-race in honour of Mars, were the last ceremonies at the close of the old Roman year.

With so many national festivals to celebrate, it is evident that the Romans did not lack excitement at any time of the year. At the end of the Republic there had been 66 days devoted to games, by the time of Marcus Aurelius (A.D. 161–180) there were

135, and near the end of the Empire in A.D. 354 there were 175—that is to say Romans might spend half the year at the Circus or amphitheatres. And even then, we have referred to little more than the religious festivals which were celebrated by games. There were many other festivals whose celebrations were confined to ceremonies, processions and feasting. But, although not all the Romans' festivals were accompanied by spectacles, in Imperial times they were the ones which provided the excitement of chariot racing in the great Circus and of gladiatorial combats in the amphitheatre beloved by the Roman mob.

ASTROLOGY

It is impossible to give an adequate account of all the cross currents of mixed traditional faith, ancient rites and customs, new imported religions and old superstitions flooding through Rome during a thousand years. Something must, however, be said of one superstition that became rife for a time among the governing classes and all those within range of their personal example and direct influence. This was the belief in astrology which grew in the teeth of the opposition of the old Roman aristocrats. They condemned, as a lot of nonsense, the pretence of the astrologers that they could predict the future career and fate of men from the positions of the stars at the time they were born. Early flirtations with astrology were frowned on very heavily. In 139 B.C. astrologers were expelled from the City by an order from one of the Praetors of Rome. It was not long after this time that political quarrels began to become more violent. While the leaders of Roman society were slaughtering each other in these long-drawn-out conflicts, the slave population of the City and the Empire was rapidly increasing and the City masses, probably for this very reason, were less and less able to see any hope of improving their poverty-stricken lives. Astrology and other superstitions had a fertile field among these poor ignorant folk. Farm bailiffs were warned not to consult the itinerant astrologers and fortune tellers, whose modest charges Cicero suggested should be deducted from the wealth they were so ready to promise to their deluded clients. Before long the Roman aristocrats themselves began to take an increasing interest in astrology.

It was not until the third century of our era that the first signs of a serious decline in the power of astrologers began to appear. Before that happened astrology had survived centuries of trial and much error. A few rare and courageous minds such as Favorinus of Arles, although a friend of the Emperor Hadrian, openly opposed fatalistic astrology with all the arguments that Cicero had exerted against it a hundred years or more earlier. Such enlightened folk were too few to make much impression. Emperors, alarmed for their personal safety, were ready to believe anything their supposedly scientific astrologers told them. As an alternative to religious impulse and inspiration, astrology was even less effective than the doctrines of Greek philosophy and theosophy to which many of the more reflective Romans tended to turn. For the masses, neither astrology nor philosophy could make any headway in competition with the attractions of the simpler superstitions of the Egyptian cult of Isis and Osiris, of Mithraism, and other Eastern mysticisms, which had been flooding into the City.

MYSTERY CULTS
Isis and Osiris

The Egyptian cult of the mother goddess Isis, goddess of the earth, of wheat and barley, whose symbolic image was a young cow, came to Rome at the beginning of the first century B.C. She was soon honoured by a statue on the Capitol, but this did not long survive, for the Senate decreed its removal. The people tried to get it back, but in 53 B.C. the chapels of Isis were destroyed and private worship of her was forbidden. As no workman would touch her shrine, the Consul himself had to demolish it. Cleopatra's presence in Rome from 46 to 44 B.C. no doubt led to renewed interest in Isis. When Augustus became Emperor in 27 B.C. Cleopatra had long been associated with his enemy Antony, so he had no wish to see reverence paid to any Egyptian goddess. Despite Augustus, however, the Temple of Isis retained its allure. Ovid makes it clear that it was popular with young women for he advises love-lorn swains to linger near it in the hope of making their acquaintance.

Domitian, who before he became Emperor had once escaped his enemies in the sacred vestments of a priest of Isis, rebuilt her temple on the *Campus Martius* on a grand scale. With her worship was associated that of Serapis (or Sarapis), chief god among the deities of Egypt. The Temple of Isis and Serapis was in the *Campus Martius* and the Temple of Serapis between it and the Forum of Trajan. Osiris, who in Egypt represented the dead Pharaoh as lord of the underworld, tended to replace Serapis in the Roman cult, where he was accepted as the spouse of Isis. Tacitus refers to the confusion between the two, saying of Serapis that 'many regard the god himself as identical with Aesculapius, because he cures the sick; some as Osiris, the oldest god among these peoples; still more identify him with Jupiter as the supreme lord of all things'. The belief in these strange deities was hallowed by their immemorial antiquity reaching far back beyond the history of Greece and Rome. It touched deeper chords of emotion, ecstacy and religious communion than could the matter-of-fact Roman State religion.

Mithraism

More powerful than any of the mystery religions of the East was the influence exerted by Mithraism in the first two centuries of the Roman Empire. As Isis and Osiris were the product of the ancient civilisation of Egypt, so the cult of Mithra(*84*), the divinity of Celestial Light, came to Rome from the equally ancient civilisations of Vedic India, of the Hittites and of Persia.

What gave Mithraism its strongest appeal were its doctrines of the immortality of the soul, the resurrection of the body and the belief that, through Mithra's help, those faithful to him would reach heaven. Meanwhile the faithful were pledged to good moral conduct, brotherly regard and mutual help, regardless of their social standing. Slaves and manual workers might stand higher in the congregation than members of old aristocratic families, for

84 Part of a Mithraic altar: Mithra slaying a bull

Mithra was the friend and champion of the poor. Like Christianity, Mithraism began as the religion of the poor and degraded servile classes and it was not until the second century A.D. that it was taken up by the Imperial Court and the educated classes.

There were little underground 'chapels', grottoes or caves dedicated to his service all over Rome, many being in private houses. They were underground, it is believed, so as to symbolise the burial from which the God would rescue the faithful. Similar little cells have been discovered in many parts of the former Roman Empire where Roman legions had been stationed. The discovery of a small temple in London a few years ago excited wide interest. Mithraism was predominantly a soldier's religion, especially in Dacia between the Carpathians and the Danube, but many other Romans such as the Imperial messengers and officials became converts.

The small size of Mithra's underground cells seems to rule out anything in the nature of congregational worship in the Christian sense; the largest would not allow of a membership of more than about one hundred. It seems certain that the ceremonies of Mithraic worship were conducted by professional clergy speaking in Greek and reading from sacred books. What was said during the complicated religious ritual, and what it may have meant, is not known.

It was the rise of Christianity that necessarily doomed Mithraism and all other pagan cults to extinction. The cult of Mithraism was vulnerable because women were not admitted and because its elaborate initiation rites further limited the number of its adherents. With the triumph of Christianity after the conversion of the Emperor Constantine in 312 A.D., the days of Mithraism were numbered, although it lingered on for several decades here and there. The full force and influence of these Eastern mystery religions represented a tremendous stirring in men's minds which seems a sign of the discontent and dissatisfaction of the times. They prepared the way for Christianity.

THE RISE OF CHRISTIANITY

It was therefore amid a welter of traditional beliefs, superstitions and newer, elaborate, ritualistic ceremonies that the simple message of the Christian gospel had to make its way. How it slowly began to do so, as the message brought by the disciples of

Jesus was welcomed and accepted as a new way of life, has been the theme of countless volumes. For the first 200 years of our era the Christians had already begun to be recognised as a new force in Roman life. So direct was their challenge to all other creeds, rites and doctrines that they were inevitably regarded, or misinterpreted, as the enemies of all religion and culture. Pliny the Younger, a typically correct, cautious and timid civil servant, reported his perplexities, when he was Roman Governor in Bithynia, to his master the Emperor Trajan. He had tortured two women slaves to 'extort the real truth about Christianity', but all he could discover 'was evidence of an absurd and extravagant superstition'. 'Great numbers of all ranks, ages and of both sexes were liable to be involved, for this contagious superstition is not confined to the cities but has spread its infection in the villages and country.' Trajan replied telling Pliny not to go out of his way to look for Christians, but he had to say that any brought in must be punished unless they recanted. The real crime of the Christians in the eyes of the State was that they met together without permission and that they refused to worship the gods. These offences against very old and settled laws of the State could not be overlooked.

As the old way of life increasingly lost its inspiration and vigour and as the eternal round of self-indulgence began to pall, Christianity grew steadily in strength by striking a fresh note, with its teaching of mercy, gentleness, loving-kindness and

85 Part of the sarcophagus of a Christian and his wife, showing Christ the Good Shepherd

charity towards others, even towards enemies; with its spurning of the world and worldly satisfactions; with its gospel of self-restraint, discipline and sobriety; with its care for the down-trodden, despised and rejected classes; with its belief in the evil of sin, the need for regeneration; with its scorn of the idols, the statues, the temples, festivals and rites with which the motley collection of Roman gods and goddesses were worshipped and for all of whom it substituted a faith in one God, the Saviour of mankind. If it echoed, in some of its teaching, ideas that were also to be found in the asceticism of the cult of Isis, in the fellowship and brotherly aid of Mithraism, in the belief in life after death and in the loving care of the Supreme Power which was common to both of them, it may have been helped by such beliefs to find a quicker access to men's minds.

By its spread and growth from strength to strength, Christianity forced those who clung to the old traditional pagan Roman ways to set about trying to mend them. Their efforts were in vain, for, by the end of the fourth century after A.D. 394, Christianity became the only official religion of the Roman people. Pagan rites had been forbidden some ten years earlier, now their colleges of priests were dissolved, and the statues of their gods and goddesses were removed.

Pagan traditions and the popular faith in Mithraism were, however, too deeply engrained to be disposed of easily, so for some long time thereafter both were kept alive, even though in secret. And the tenacity of Roman customs was such that although, with the official adoption of Christianity, the festivals of the pagan goddesses and gods were of course abolished, it did not prove at all easy to abolish gladiator fights. Denounced by philosophers and by the Fathers of the Christian Church, they were far too popular to be given up, and it was not until the beginning of the fifth century A.D., when the barbarians were bursting through the Imperial defences, that the Emperor Honorius decreed the abolition of gladiatorial combats. Horrors and slaughter in unending succession were at last halted, soon however to be recommenced by the barbarians themselves, no longer as the victims, as the slaves, prisoners and gladiators slaughtered in the arenas to make a Roman holiday, but now as invaders, butchers, looters and destroyers swarming into Italy and surging over the newly erected defences of Rome and leaving

194

such havoc and desolation in their wake that Imperial Rome slowly sank into hopeless ruin and decay. The very site of the great temple of Jupiter which had for a thousand years been the supreme shrine of the Roman people through all the striking vicissitudes of their fate, was overlaid on the Capitoline hill and its place forgotten. Its fate may symbolise the collapse and extinction of Rome, and the belated fulfilment of the prophetic vision of Scipio Aemilianus in 146 B.C. as, with tears in his eyes, he watched the flames devouring proud Carthage, the Phoenician capital he had been commanded to capture and to destroy. 'This, he thought,' said Polybius who stood by his side, 'had befallen Ilium, once a powerful city, and the once mighty empires of the Assyrians, Medes, Persians and that of Macedonia, lately so splendid. And unintentionally or purposely he quoted (from the *Illiad* of Homer), the words perhaps escaping him unconsciously,

The day shall be when holy Troy shall fall
And Priam, lord of spears, and Priam's folk.'

CHRONOLOGICAL SUMMARY

Chronological tables for the entire history of Rome are given in *A Companion to Latin Studies* (C.U.P., 1929) and the *Cambridge Ancient History*, vols. VII–XII. For the Empire alone neither is as full as the *Chronologie de l'Empire Romain* by G. Goyau (Paris, 1891).

THE REPUBLIC

B.C. 753   Founding of Rome by Romulus: first year of Roman chronology

509   Expulsion of Etruscan kings and foundation of Republic

Fifth Century   *Defensive Wars of Rome.*

450   Laws of the Twelve Tables

Fourth Century *Wars of expansion: Rome supreme in central Italy. Plebeians achieve legal equality with Patricians.*

Third Century   *Rome supreme throughout Italy. Beginnings of foreign conquest.*

268   First divorce in Rome

264   First exhibition of Gladiators

264–241   First Punic War

219   First Greek physician in Rome

Ennius (239–169)

218–202   Second Punic War: defeat of Hannibal

Plautus (251–184)

Second Century *Imperialist expansion in Greece, Middle East, Spain and N. Africa. Influence of Greek culture on Roman life and literature.*

185   Senate forbids permanent theatre

184   Censorship of Elder Cato (234–149)

167   Greek historian Polybius in Rome

Terence (194–159)

161   Philosophers and rhetoricians expelled

155   Three Greek philosophers in Rome

149–146   Destruction of Carthage

139   Chaldaean fortune-tellers expelled

Accius (170–86)

134–132   First Slave War

133–121   Gracchan Reforms

B.C.	103–2	Second Slave War
	102	Marius defeats Teutones and reorganises the Roman Army
First Century		*Wars in the East. Civil War in Italy. Collapse of Republic.*
	91–88	Social War
	90–82	Civil War: Marius *v.* Sulla
	81–79	Dictatorship of Sulla
	73–71	Third Slave War: Spartacus' revolt
	70	Pompey and Crassus weaken Sullan constitution
	67–63	Pompey's conquests in East Cicero (106–43)
	63	Consulship of Cicero Lucretius (96–55)
	62	Defeat of Catiline Catullus (82–52)
	59	Consulship of Julius Caesar (100–44)
		Sallust (87–35)
	58	Free corn-dole for 320,000 Romans
	58–49	Caesar's conquest of Gaul Virgil (70–19)
	44	Civil War follows Caesar's assassination
		Tibullus (48–19)
	31	Battle of Actium ends Civil War
		Propertius (50–10)
	27	Augustus establishes one-man rule and creates Praetorian Guard Horace (65–8)

THE EMPIRE

Julio-Claudian Emperors

B.C.	27	Augustus
A.D.	9	Defeat of Varus in Teutoburg forest
		Livy (59 B.C.–A.D. 17)
	10	Rhine defences organised Ovid (43 B.C.–A.D. 17)
	14	Death and deification of Augustus
	14	Tiberius
	16	Extension of frontier to Elbe abandoned
	29	Crucifixion of Jesus
	37	Caligula Seneca (5–65)
	41	Claudius Petronius (*d.* 65)
	54	Nero Elder Pliny (23–79)
	64	Great fire of Rome Lucan (39–65)
	69	Year of Four Emperors

Flavian Emperors

	69	Vespasian Quintilian (35–95)
	70	Capture of Jerusalem by Titus
	79	Destruction of Pompeii and Herculaneum

A.D.	79	Titus	Martial (46–104)
	81	Domitian	Tacitus (55–120)
	96	Nerva	Younger Pliny (62–113)

Spanish Emperors

	98	Trajan	Juvenal (*c.* 50–127)
	117	Hadrian	Suetonius (69–140)

Antonine Emperors

	138	Antoninus Pius	
	161	Marcus Aurelius	Apuleius (*b.* 123)
	180	Greatest expansion of Empire	
	180	Commodus	

North African and Syrian Emperors

	193	Septimius Severus	Tertullian (*fl.* 200)
	211	Caracalla	
	218	Elagabalus	
	222	Severus Alexander	
	235	Military anarchy	
	284	Diocletian and the Tetrarchy	

Dynasty of Constantine (305–363)

	312	Battle of the Mulvian Bridge
	312	Praetorian Guard disbanded
	313	Edict favouring Christians
	337	Death of Constantine
	361	Julian
	362	Paganism restored
	363	Death of Julian

Dynasty of Valentinian and Theodosius (364–394)

	364	Valentinian	Ammianus Marcellinus
	379	Theodosius	(*fl.* 390)
	391	Paganism forbidden	
			Macrobius (*fl.* 400)
	394	Christianity sole official religion	
			St. Jerome (340–420)

Fifth Century *End of the Western Empire*

	410	Capture and sack of Rome by the Visigoths
		St. Augustine (354–430)
	455	Sack of Rome by the Vandals
	472	Sack of Rome by Ricimer
	476	Odoacer deposes last Western Roman Emperor

A NOTE ABOUT BOOKS

In every generation the story of Rome and its heritage is worked over again in the light of new discoveries and from new points of view. That is why Roman history exerts its perennial fascination and why it is not something to be dropped and forgotten as soon as school and college days are over. No one volume such as this can possibly tell everything worth knowing, so the following list is given to indicate sources of information to supplement what has been said, or what has been omitted for lack of space. The first priority in wider reading should be the works of the old Roman authors, most of which have been translated, in series such as the Loeb Library. The chief general works of reference are:

Oxford Classical Dictionary, ed. H. H. Scullard
Cambridge Ancient History, Vols. VII (1928)-XII (1939)
SMITH, W. *Dictionary of Greek and Roman Antiquities*

Special topics are treated in:
ARNOLD, E. V. *Roman Stoicism* (C.U.P., 1911)
BAILEY, C. *Ed. The Legacy of Rome* (O.U.P., 1923)
    Ed. The Mind of Rome (O.U.P., 1926)
BALSDON, J. P. V. D. *Life and Leisure in Ancient Rome* (Bodley Head, 1969)
BANDINELLI, R. B. *Rome/Roman Art to* A.D. *200; Roman Art* A.D. *200–400*, trs. Green, P., 2 vols. (Thames and Hudson, 1970–71)
BEARE, W. *The Roman Stage* (Methuen, 1968)
BIGOT, P. *Rome antique au 4ᵉᵐᵉ siècle* (Vincent, Fréal, Paris, 1955)
BOETHIUS, A. *The Golden House of Nero* (Cresset Press, 1960) and WARD-PERKINS, J. B. *Etruscan and Roman Architecture* (Penguin, 1970)
BUTLER, A. J. *Sport in Classic Times* (Benn, 1930)
BRUNT, P. A. *Roman Manpower* (O.U.P., 1971); *Social Conflicts in the Roman Republic* (Chatto and Windus, 1971)
CARCOPINO, J. *Daily Life in Ancient Rome* (Routledge & Kegan Paul, 1941; Penguin Books, 1956)
COCHRANE, C. N. *Christianity and Classical Culture* (O.U.P., 1957)
COWELL, F. R. *Cicero and the Roman Republic* (Pitman, 1948; Penguin, 6th ed., 1972)
CRAMER, F. H. *Astrology in Roman Law and Politics* (American Philosophical Society, 1954)
CROOK, J. A. *Law and Life of Rome* (Thames and Hudson, 1967)
DAUBE, D. *Roman Law* (Edinburgh University Press, 1969)
DILL, SIR S. *Roman Society from Nero to Marcus Aurelius* (Macmillan, 1905); *Roman Society in the last century of the Western Empire* (Macmillan, 1925)

DRACHMANN, A. G. *Mechanical Technology of Greek and Roman Antiquity* (Copenhagen, 1963)

DUDLEY, D. R. *Urbs Roma* (Phaidon, 1967)

DUFF, A. M. *Freedmen in the Early Roman Empire* (O.U.P., 1928)

EARL, D. *The Moral and Political Tradition of Rome* (Thames and Hudson, 1967)

FERGUSON, J. *The Religions of the Roman Empire* (Thames and Hudson, 1970)

FINLEY, M. I., ed. *Slavery in Classical Antiquity* (Heffer, 1960)

FLOWER, B. and ROSENBAUM, E. *The Roman Cookery Book* (Harrap, 1958)

FORBES, R. J. *Studies in Ancient Technology.* Eleven vols. (Brill Leiden, 1955–64).

FOWLER, W. W. *Social Life at Rome in the Age of Cicero* (Macmillan, 1908); *The Religious Experience of the Roman People* (Macmillan, 1911); *Roman Ideas of Deity* (Macmillan, 1914); *Roman Festivals* (Macmillan, 1899)

FRANK, TENNEY. *An Economic Survey of Ancient Rome*, 5 vols. (O.U.P., 1933–40); *Life and Literature in the Roman Republic* (C.U.P., 1930); *Aspects of Social Behaviour in Ancient Rome* (O.U.P., 1932)

FRIEDLANDER, L. *Roman Life and Manners under the Early Empire.* Four vols. (Routledge & Kegan Paul, 1940)

GARDINER, E. N. *Athletics in the Ancient World* (O.U.P., 1955)

GEIKIE, SIR A. *The Love of Nature among the Romans* (Murray, 1912)

GRANT, M. *The World of Rome* (Weidenfeld and Nicolson, 1960); *Myths of the Greeks and Romans* (Weidenfeld and Nicolson, 1962); (*Ed.*) *The Birth of Western Civilisation* (Thames and Hudson, 1964)

GRIMAL, P. *Les Jardins Romains* (Les Presses Universitaires, 1969)

HAARHOFF, T. *Schools of Gaul* (Witwatersrand University, 1958) *The Stranger within the Gate* (Longmans, 1938)

HANDS, A. R. *Charities and Social Aid in Greece and Rome* (Thames and Hudson, 1968)

HIGGINS, R. H. *Greek and Roman Jewellery* (Methuen, 1961)

HILL, H. *The Roman Middle Class, Republican Period* (Blackwell, 1952)

JENNISON, G. *Animals for Show and Pleasure in Ancient Rome* (Manchester University Press, 1937)

JONES, A. H. M. *The Decline of the Ancient World* (Longmans, 1966)

KENYON, SIR F. G. *Books and Readers in Ancient Greece and Rome* (O.U.P., 1932)

LINTOTT, A. W. *Violence in Republican Rome* (O.U.P., 1968)

MCDONALD, A. H. *Republican Rome* (Thames and Hudson, 1966)

MAIURI, A. *Roman Painting* (Skira edn., Zwemmer, 1953) *Pompeii* (Instituto Geografico de Agostini, 1957)

MARGARY, I. D. *Roman Roads in Britain*, 2 vols (J. Baker, 1967)

MARROU, H. I. *History of Education in Antiquity* (Sheed and Ward, 1956)

MEIGGS, R. *Roman Ostia* (O.U.P., 1969)

MOMIGLIANO, A. D. Ed. *Paganism and Christianity—4th Century* (Oxford Warburg, 1963)

MORITZ, L. A. *Grain Mills and Flour in Classical Antiquity* (O.U.P., 1958)

NASH, E. *Pictorial Dictionary of Ancient Rome*, 2 vols. (Thames and Hudson, 1968)

OGILVIE R. M. *The Romans and their Gods* (Chatto and Windus, 1969)

PAOLI, U. E. *Rome, Its People, Life and Customs* (Longmans, 1963)

POLLITT, J. J. *The Art of Rome* c. 753 B.C.–A.D. 337. Sources and Documents (Prentice-Hall, 1966)

RICHTER, G. M. A. *The Furniture of the Greeks, Etruscans and Romans* (Phaidon, 1966)

Roman Lettering, Victoria and Albert Museum (H.M.S.O., 1958)

ROSE, H. J. *Handbook of Latin Literature* (Methuen, 1966)

SCARBOROUGH, J. *Roman Medicine* (Thames and Hudson, 1969)

SCULLARD, H. H. *The Etruscan Cities and Rome* (Thames and Hudson, 1967)

SELTMAN, C. *Wine in the Ancient World* (Routledge, 1957)

SHERWIN-WHITE, A. N. *Racial Prejudice in Imperial Rome* (C.U.P., 1967)

STAHL. *Roman Science* (University of Wisconsin, 1962)

STAVELEY, E. S. *Greek and Roman Voting and Elections* (Thames and Hudson, 1970)

STENICO, A. *Roman and Etruscan Painting* (Weidenfeld and Nicolson, 1963)

SYME, SIR R. *The Roman Revolution* (O.U.P., 1939 and 1960)

TOYNBEE, JOCELYN, *Roman Art* (Thames and Hudson, 1965); *Death and Burial in the Roman World* (Thames and Hudson, 1971)

TREGGIARI, SUSAN, *Roman Freedmen during the Late Republic* (O.U.P., 1969)

VOGT, J. *The Decline of Rome* (Weidenfeld and Nicolson, 1967)

WALBANK, F. W. *The Awful Revolution. Decline of the Roman Empire* (Liverpool University Press, 1969)

WATSON, A. *Roman Law in the Later Roman Republic* (O.U.P., 1967–71)

WATSON, G. R. *The Roman Soldier* (Thames and Hudson, 1969)

WHITE, K. D. *Agricultural Implements in the Roman World* (C.U.P., 1967); *Roman Farming* (Thames and Hudson, 1970)

WILKINSON, L. P. *Horace and his Lyric Poetry* (C.U.P., 1945); *Ovid Recalled* (C.U.P., 1958); *Golden Latin Artistry* (C.U.P., 1963)

INDEX

The numerals in **bold type** refer to the figure numbers of the illustrations